Landscaping Decks, Patios & Balconies

Created and designed by
the editorial staff of
ORTHO BOOKS

Project Editor
Sara M. Shopkow

Writer
Sara Godwin

Illustrator
Lois Lovejoy

Designer
Gary Hespenheide

Ortho Books

Publisher
Robert B. Loperena

Editorial Director
Christine Jordan

Manufacturing Manager
Ernie S. Tasaki

Editors
Robert J. Beckstrom
Michael D. Smith

Managing Editor
Sally W. Smith

Prepress Supervisor
Linda M. Bouchard

Editorial Assistants
Joni Christiansen
Sally J. French

Address all inquiries to:
Ortho Books
Box 5006
San Ramon, CA 94583-0906

Copyright © 1994
Monsanto Company
All rights reserved under international and Pan-American copyright conventions.

2	3	4	5	6	7	8	9
95		96	97	98	99		

ISBN 0-89721-266-5
Library of Congress Catalog Card Number 93-86236

THE SOLARIS GROUP
2527 Camino Ramon
San Ramon, CA 94583

Acknowledgments

Consultant
Steven Still

Photography Editor
Judy Mason

Editorial Coordinator
Cass Dempsey

Copyeditor
Toni Murray

Proofreader
David Sweet

Indexer
Patricia Feuerstein

Layout by
Indigo Design & Imaging

Separations by
Color Tech Corp.

Lithographed in the USA by
Banta Company

Special Thanks to
Deborah Cowder
Elizabeth and David Nelson

Photographers
Names of photographers are followed by the page numbers on which their work appears.
R = right, C = center, L = left, T = top, B = bottom.

Baker: 75R, 86
Liz Ball/Photo/NATS: 63R
Laurie Black: 30, 76BR
John Blaustein: 14, back cover TR
Margarite Bradley/Positive Images: 8, 80R
Patricia Bruno/Positive Images: 23L, 39, 46B
Karen Bussolini/Positive Images: 26, 53T, 68L
Josephine Coatsworth: 28–29
Candace Cochrane/Positive Images: 31T
COMSTOCK: 70B
Townsend Dickinson/COMSTOCK: 68R
Derek Fell: 4–5, 6, 13B, 15T, 25, 31B, 32, 45TR, 50, 61T, 64B, 72L, 73T, 83R, 85, 88, back cover TL
Margaret Hensel/Positive Images: title page, 9, 12, 61B, 62, 66L, 67T
Jerry Howard/Positive Images: 7, 10–11, 16, 17, 18, 19, 23R, 45TL, 45BR, 46T, 48, 51L, 52, 53B, 54B, 58, 59, 63L, 64T, 64C, 67B, 72R, 73B, 75L, 76BL, 78R, 83L, 87, 93, back cover BL & BR
Sydney Karp/Photo/NATS: 76T, 82B
Michael Landis: 80L, 90
Lee Lockwood/Positive Images: 13T, 42–43, 54T, 66R, 69R, 70T, 92
Robert Lyons/Photo/NATS: 24
Ivan Masser/Positive Images: 22, 57R, 74
Michael McKinley: 57L
OIS: 13C, 44, 51R, 55, 56, 77, 78L, 81R, 82T, 82C, 91B
Paul Rezendes/Positive Images: 27, 45BL, 69L
Kenneth Rice: front cover
Michael S. Thompson/COMSTOCK: 21, 49, 65
Tracey: 89
Jeff Williams: 15B
Marilyn Wood/Photo/NATS: 71

Front Cover
Permanent plantings in built-ins, bright annuals and a rose in colorful pots, and greenery set directly in the ground are all part of the landscaping for this deck.

Title Page
An atmosphere created by just the right furniture and plants invites you to linger.

Back Cover
Top left: Well-established shrubs and trees shelter an intimate patio in an urban backyard.

Top right: A tiny balcony can be a lush spot for reading.

Bottom left: A formal pairing of containers brings lively color to a lattice pergola.

Bottom right: Container gardening can include vegetables as well as flowers.

Landscaping Decks, Patios & Balconies

Combining Outdoors and Indoors

The dividing line between home and garden is vanishing. More than ever, people try to combine the elements of both interior and exterior for their outdoor spaces.

This is a book about the parts of a garden you live in, about outdoor "rooms." It is about decks, patios, and balconies that act as extensions of the house and serve many of the same functions as the rooms in your home. This book applies to these areas the same considerations you bring to decorating your bedroom or living room. It is a book about style and taste, but also about practical things, such as getting water to a hanging fuchsia and how big a container you need to hold a lemon tree.

Patios, decks, and balconies usually adjoin the house; they are areas occupants can go to as easily as they pass from one room of the house to another. Often such an area shares the function of the room it adjoins or has a related function. A deck off a kitchen might be a favorite dining area in fine weather; a tiny private balcony off a bedroom may be a personal retreat. Somehow a party seems more like an occasion when guests can spill out of the living room and onto the deck or patio and perhaps into the garden as well.

Because these outdoor rooms function like their indoor counterparts, they should be furnished with the same care, the same attention to taste and style, as the interior of the house. When outdoor space is as comfortable as indoor space, you may find that you prefer to spend your leisure hours on the patio, basking in the sun or reading, instead of watching television indoors.

An urban courtyard becomes a hidden garden. This quiet retreat is brilliant with azaleas in the spring and a cool green during the heat of summer.

CONSIDERING OUTDOOR LIVING SPACES

Outdoor rooms on decks and patios are for doing all the things that are done indoors—sitting, talking, reading, eating—and more. The biggest difference is the pleasure of doing them in the open air, surrounded by greenery, flowers, and fragrance. In a world where living spaces seem to get nothing but smaller, outdoor living is more important and more appealing than ever.

A sun porch, screened-in porch, or verandah is a special kind of outdoor room, a hybrid of indoors and outdoors. Each of these rooms has a roof, floor, and walls and is also open to the air. These spaces are generally furnished more like real rooms than decks and patios are. They are wonderful places for wicker, bamboo, or rattan furniture, which needs more protection from rain and sun than decks or patios can offer. A sun porch may be home to a wicker plant stand filled with trailing bird's-foot ivy or

a fern stand with a huge Boston fern in all its magnificence. A screened-in porch makes a particularly pleasant summer retreat, especially when the space contains baskets of tuberous begonias, fuchsias, impatiens, or ferns hung from the ceiling and sweet peas or hops climbing the outside posts.

Plants on a deck or around a patio can accomplish any number of worthwhile objectives. Pots of bright color can create an attractive view from the house; a hedge in a long planter can screen out an unattractive view. Use a small fountain or waterfall to mask the sounds of traffic. Potted trees can provide everything from shade to privacy to fruit, and planters can help establish traffic patterns by defining paths. They can highlight an entryway or divide an eating area, where adults want peace and quiet, from the children's play area. Landscaped decks, patios, and other outdoor areas make any house or apartment more livable and more enjoyable.

CREATING A PARADISE THROUGH DESIGN

Is the outdoor room to be elegant or casual? Do you want a lush jungle of greenery or the Zen simplicity of three perfect bonsai? Will guests nibble on dainty sandwiches at high tea or will the neighborhood kids play space explorers? Style may be casual or formal, elegant or rustic, witty or traditional. A fountain, for example, may be in the traditional tiled style of a Spanish courtyard. Or, you might prefer a simple stone urn perpetually overflowing its mossy sides; a wall-mounted version of the mask of comedy, pouring water into a small basin; or a waterfall tumbling over rocks. Garden sculpture may range from terra-cotta bunnies to marble torsos, from contemporary metal sculpture to concrete greyhounds holding baskets of flowers in their mouths, from garden leprechauns to painted wooden ducks with wings that whirl in the wind. Each has its own style.

The same is true of the containers used for planting. From bas-relief urns to brightly painted Mexican pots, from Versailles boxes to Chinese egg jars, from porcelain blue-and-white oriental pots to old-fashioned terra-cotta flowerpots, there are a myriad of choices. Each creates a different mood.

Top: A small urban deck can be used as an extension of the house or apartment. Bottom: The simple furnishings and plant arrangement of this latticed pergola allow attention to focus on the greenery beyond.

Plants are as important as furniture and decorations in creating mood. A deck furnished with Japanese maples, camellias, azaleas, lily-of-the-valley shrub, and heavenly bamboo would have an oriental flavor even if the owner did not intend it. A patio with big pots of olive trees; smaller pots of oleander, bougainvillea, star-jasmine, and rosemary; and a grapevine-covered arbor creates the ambience of a Mediterranean villa.

This book will help you choose sculpture, containers, plants, and other decorations that contribute to the effect you desire. The challenge is to coordinate all the diverse elements to create a unity of style that ultimately reflects the taste and activities of the people who use the outdoor room. Victorian cast-iron chairs look ill at ease with a redwood picnic table. An American folk-art whirligig strikes an amusing note on a patio furnished with rustic bent-willow furniture; it seems obtrusive on a terrace furnished with Japanese stone lanterns and bonsai.

It is equally crucial that pots and planters, trees and flowers, and furniture and decorations be in proportion with the size of the space.

This garden combines three elements—brick, poppies, and a central sculpture—to create an unaffected ambience.

Obviously, the more space that is given over to furniture, the less space there is for plants, and vice versa. The key is this: A well-proportioned outdoor room feels comfortable. There is space to walk without barking a shin on the table or catching a sleeve on the roses. There is a place to lay down a book or the Sunday paper without knocking over the flowers. A guest can walk under the eaves without bumping into the hanging basket or the bird feeder.

The whole purpose of an outdoor room is to create a sense of ineluctable luxury. A Japanese garden designer once said that the key to design is to pare away everything that does not belong until everything that remains does belong. The same principle is true of garden design, deck and patio design, and life.

USING THIS BOOK

This book is organized to help you approach the design of an outdoor room in a logical, informed way. The discussion begins by presenting concepts—design principles and aesthetic considerations. Because the selection of the plants is usually the aspect of design that involves the most factors, the second chapter

A gathering of wrought-iron chairs is shaded by a clematis amidst a lush profusion of plants.

ends by emphasizing the plant selection process. From there the information becomes more specific. You will learn practical considerations about the long-term care of plants and how to select healthy specimens. The fourth chapter, "Selecting Your Scene," presents a collection of design examples. Each serves a distinct purpose or evokes a specific mood. The descriptions of the designs contain the common names and Latin names of plants as well as details about the placement of plants, furnishings, and decorations. If the design suits your climate, you could certainly adopt it as presented and bring it to life on your deck, patio, or balcony. Probably, however, you will adapt a design, using the parts that are most suitable to your environment and life-style. Use this book as an idea resource. With what you will learn in the first three chapters about design, plant selection, and your own environment and goals, you should have no trouble choosing elements from the sample designs that will help you achieve an outdoor room that is a continual pleasure.

Understanding the Elements of Design

Once you decide how you want to use an outdoor room, you must furnish the space appropriately. This chapter discusses the aspects of design that a professional would consider in creating a distinctive and appealing space.

Just as bedrooms have beds, libraries have bookshelves, and dining rooms have dining tables, decks and patios should have the furnishings and plants that best serve their primary purpose. A balcony can be a quiet retreat if it has a big comfortable chair to curl up in and fragrant, flowering vines twining up the walls to create a bower. Entertaining the neighbors on the lanai at weekend barbecues requires, besides the barbecue, a table and chairs. When the pool deck is the staging area for teenagers' swim parties, you'll need a safe electrical outlet to plug in the inevitable music, a table to serve food, and a place to throw wet towels.

Some outdoor spaces must serve more than one purpose. The patio may be the place where the cook grows the kitchen herbs, the avid gardener tends the cherished climbing roses, and toddlers can play within sight and earshot of those in the house. Achieving such a multiuse area is easy enough if a sunny, narrow border is given over to the herbs, an arbor or arch is built for the roses, and sufficient level space is allotted for a sandbox and swing.

A fresh perspective can help you take advantage of existing design elements.

A properly designed entryway harmonizes with the home, directing visitors to the door with maximum grace and minimum fuss.

By now you must be convinced: The most important question to ask yourself in planning your outdoor room is how you would like to use the space. A little more introspection is required, however, before you begin to create the deck or patio of your dreams. Look deep into your heart and determine exactly how much work you are willing to do to maintain the outdoor area. Do you have the energy and inclination to empty the hanging baskets each fall and replant them again in spring? Do you have time every morning to fill bird feeders with fresh seed and the birdbath with clean water? An overly ambitious outdoor area strewn with dead and dying plants, empty bird feeders, and broken chairs is a sorry sight.

THE DESIGNER'S PALETTE

To turn a vision into a reality, the designer of an outdoor room considers and manipulates a number of factors. These include landscaping; proportion, texture, and color; architecture; lighting; and furnishings. The designer must also consider whether nature can make a contribution. For example, would the evening visit of a hummingbird be the finishing touch? Would the scene seem incomplete without the visits of a squirrel?

Landscaping

When it comes to decks, patios, and balconies, landscaping includes more than selecting appropriate plants. It also encompasses choosing practical containers that will contribute to the design of the outdoor room and including decorative elements large and small—from a rushing stream to a delicate wind chime.

Plants Graceful palms, big-leafed philodendrons, and thickly flowered vines can make a suburban deck seem like an equatorial rain forest. Tall cactuses, intricately patterned succulents, and the delicate shadows of palo verde trees on a patio suggest the mysteries of the desert. In each case, the choice of plants determines a distinct atmosphere. The designs in the fourth chapter, "Selecting Your Scene," will provide more examples that will give you a sense of the moods specific plants evoke.

Containers Pots and planters also contribute to the mood and style of an outdoor room. White Versailles planter boxes provide a formal, elegant, and traditional ambience; old half-barrels contribute to an atmosphere that is informal and simple.

Mood is not the only factor to keep in mind when choosing a container. Consider whether the container complements the plant you are planning to place into it. A carefully clipped and manicured bay tree might look out of place in an old wine barrel; a rambunctious, tousled asparagus fern may seem inappropriate in a white Versailles box. In addition, consider the size of the plant. Large plants, such as trees or substantial shrubs, need large pots to balance their size. Small planters, such as window boxes, need small plants whose flowers don't overwhelm them. Pots and plants look best when they are appropriate to each other. (See Choosing Containers, in the third chapter, for a discussion that includes practical as well as aesthetic tips about container selection.)

Decorative elements   One of the most appealing decorative elements is water. Water seems like a living thing, offering a soothing sound and a fascinating play of light. Even the smallest garden can present the pleasure of water. The grimiest air shaft in Manhattan can have Boston ivy or climbing hydrangea growing up the wall to cling around a lion's-head wall fountain. The smallest balcony can accommodate a half-barrel planted with papyrus and a single waterlily. A Japanese garden seems complete with the addition of a mossy stone basin filled from a trickling bamboo pipe. A small waterfall that spills into a lighted pool of fragrant night-blooming waterlilies is magical at night.

As you plan your outdoor room, consider whether including a fountain, pool, stream, or waterfall is appropriate and possible. (See Wondrous Water Gardens, in the fourth chapter, to learn about practical considerations.) If one of these elements already exists, arrange plants, seating, lighting, and the like to maximize your enjoyment of them.

Don't overlook arches and trellises as you think of ways to decorate your outdoor room. Planted with vines, climbing roses, or espaliered fruit trees, an arch or trellis can bring beauty to overhead space or a barren wall. What's more, these practical decorations can help you define space. A trellis, for example, can serve as an outdoor wall and direct traffic into desired patterns.

The sample designs in the fourth chapter of this book include a variety of decorative elements—that is, sculpture, fixtures, and accent

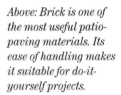

Above: Brick is one of the most useful patio-paving materials. Its ease of handling makes it suitable for do-it-yourself projects.

The eye is drawn to the single orange tree on the patio. The decorative terra-cotta pot makes a strong visual statement.

This fountain uses not-so-unusual materials to create an unusual effect. Bamboo potted in ceramics to match the fountain completes the Asian theme.

pieces. You'll find more decorative items as you wander through nurseries or thumb through garden catalogs. The range of available decoration may seem overwhelming. How do you decide what to choose? As you study the sample designs, be aware of how a decorative element contributes to the outdoor room it is a part of. By honing your sense of how decoration can support design, the pieces you'll choose will complement the overall look while adding personality to your outdoor room.

Proportion, Texture, and Color

Many decks, lanais, and balconies are small in comparison with interior rooms. Others are quite large, as when an entire yard is bricked or cobbled as a patio. For these spaces to seem comfortable, all the elements must be in proportion to each other. On a narrow condominium balcony, one chaise lounge may well take up all the room there is. A more practical choice might be a little French bistro table with a pair of chairs; these furnishings would leave room for flowers.

Plant size is another important factor that contributes to proportion. Large-leafed plants and dense greenery create a rain-forest effect, the feel of burgeoning growth. Small-leafed plants create a feeling of controlled order. Picture a patio landscaped with tree ferns (*Gunnera tinctoria*), whose leaves are up to 8 feet

across, and pink and white caladium; now picture the same patio landscaped with cut-leaf maple, azaleas, and Japanese iris.

A collection of large potted shrubs can easily make a compact patio feel crowded. A better selection might be a rotating collection of annuals that are set into permanent cachepots and changed with each season. Plant burgundy chrysanthemums in October, red poinsettias in December, pink florist's cyclamen in January, yellow daffodils in March, white marguerites in May, dark-blue dwarf delphiniums in August, and chrysanthemums again in autumn. Or, using the same flowers, create an all-white garden by choosing white cultivars of each of the species.

On a very large deck or patio, small pots of annual color may be too small to have any effect whatsoever. In such a case, half-barrels overflowing with herbs not only smell good, but are big enough to have some impact. A dramatic herb barrel could contain dill, lovage, or angelica in the center; parsley in a circle around it; and a variety of mints (peppermint, spearmint, orange mint, pennyroyal, for example) tumbling over the edges. A perennial version of this (and one requiring less water) might have a large pineapple sage in the center, garden sage in a circle around it, winter savory in a second circle, and dwarf rosemary set along the edges to trail over the sides in a thick curtain of green.

Left: Like a blank canvas, this empty balcony awaits completion.
Right: The same balcony, transformed into what might well become the most used room in the house. The abundance of plants makes it cozy.

Texture and color also play a role in establishing proportion. Rough textures, such as herringbone brick, and dark colors, such as black urethane, seem to contract space. Smooth surfaces, such as steel-troweled concrete, and light colors, such as the silvery gray of weathered redwood, make space seem larger. Enclosed space, such as a walled courtyard, seems smaller than space open to a long, wide view.

Architecture

Some architectural styles have landscaping styles to match. Mediterranean-style houses almost demand brilliantly flowering bougainvillea vines clambering up the walls and along the eaves. Brick houses look richly traditional when thickly covered with Boston ivy. Shingle-style cottages seem to require climbing roses or morning glories at doorways or on garden gates.

The fact that some architectures and landscaping styles are traditional partners doesn't mean that they must always be used together, however. Breaking traditional formulas may result in a wonderfully innovative outdoor room. A New York brownstone with a patio decorated with sculptural cactuses and Southwestern furniture looks witty rather than classic. With white wicker furniture and antique roses in mossy basket-weave pots under an arbor of wisteria, a California ranch-style house evokes echoes of an earlier age.

Top: Although this walled passage is narrow, border shrubs and welcoming flowers make it inviting and tranquil.
Bottom: If you wish the architecture of your home to remain the focal point, all you may need are a tree for summer shade and one or two pots of color.

The advantages of wicker furniture are its lightness and the romantic ambience it creates.

Cast-iron furniture contributes a European flavor that may well be worth the work of a yearly touchup.

Lighting

Lights add tremendously to the usefulness and effect of decks and patios, especially in climates blessed with warm evenings in spring and Indian summer, times when there is limited natural daylight. Lights from the eaves or on posts can light an entire patio area. Outdoor floodlights can highlight a dramatic tree or a flower bed in full bloom. Underwater lights can make a swimming pool, fountain, or fish pond look enchanting. If there are paths or stairs leading to or from the deck or patio, lights are essential for safety. Colored lights create a dramatic effect (most floodlights can easily be fitted with colored lenses). Turning a spotlight on a sculptural plant, such as a tall cactus or a yucca, creates an attractive view that can be enjoyed from the house as well as from the deck or patio.

Furnishings

The term *furnishings* refers to more than tables and chairs. Furnishing an outdoor room may involve considering elements as diverse as umbrellas and barbecues.

Furniture   Choosing outdoor furniture can be a challenge simply because there are so many factors to consider. How it looks and what it costs may be the primary concerns, but there are many others. Can it be left out or must it be protected from rain and snow? Might it mildew? Does it need cushions and, if it does, are the cushion covers easily removable for washing?

A great deal of furniture is for the outdoors only in the sense that you'd never allow such unappealing stuff inside the house. It doesn't make a lot of sense to spend good money for patio furniture so ugly it makes you wince every time you look at it, or so flimsy it will barely make it through the summer. Until you find the sort of furniture that gives you the look and feel you're after, use wooden crates or half-barrels as low tables and drape them with bright fabrics. Top others with plump Provençal-print pillows to create chairs. These temporary furnishings will serve until you can find furniture you really want and can afford. Then, when you view the outdoor space, you will see that the effect was worth the wait.

Some kinds of patio furniture can be left outside all year long; others need to be stored for the winter. Some outdoor furniture folds or stacks so it takes up minimal room when stored; other types do neither. Heavy plastic furniture is virtually impervious to weather. Natural teak, cedar, and redwood pieces become even more beautiful as they are exposed to the elements, turning a handsome silvery gray as they age. Cast iron lasts practically forever, but rain can cause it to rust. So, to keep it attractive, be ready each spring with a can of spray paint. As an alternative to cast iron, consider aluminum. Aluminum reproductions of traditional Victorian cast-iron pieces are now available, and aluminum has the advantages of being lightweight and easy to move and refusing to rust. Painted furniture may fade, chip, or peel after a while; you may have to spend the better part of a weekend with sandpaper and paintbrush to make it look clean and fresh for the summer season. Wicker, bamboo, and rattan are charming, but they deteriorate rapidly if set out in direct sun or left out in the rain. In addition, most styles are bulky and clumsy to store. They do best on open verandahs and sun porches where they get minimum exposure to the ravages of weather. To design your own seating arrangements, consider modular slat benches and planters of natural cedar.

Outdoor tables come in a variety of styles and materials. A redwood picnic table with redwood benches is an American classic. Elaborately curlicued cast-iron tables and chairs call up visions of a Victorian lawn party. For especially small spaces, such as balconies, French bistro furniture has a wonderful Continental look and takes up very little room. Decorate a bistro table with a small pot of topiaried rosemary, spend Saturday afternoon reading an international edition of the *Herald Tribune,* sip French-roast coffee, and feel positively Parisian. The best thing about outdoor tables is that they make drinking a single cup of coffee as pleasurable as a picnic.

To ward off the sun or to keep falling leaves off a table, you need an umbrella. Umbrellas, like furniture, come in all sorts of styles. Before you buy one, be sure your table has a hole in the center to slip the umbrella pole into. There are classic café umbrellas emblazoned with "Cinzano"; there are square market-stall umbrellas of heavy canvas; there are oiled-paper umbrellas from Thailand, gaily painted with sunrises and water and storks. The different types create different looks, a difference as great as that between Paris and Bangkok.

Barbecues and fireplaces Eating outdoors is one of the special pleasures of life. When food is prepared outdoors on a barbecue, the cooking is part of the fun. Barbecues range from permanent stone or brick structures to round metal devices with wheels to small cast-iron hibachis. Grilled fish and steaks probably taste pretty much the same from any one of them, but the effect on the outdoor room is certainly very different. Handsome stone barbecues add significant value to a property, which is important to a homeowner but probably not worth the investment to a renter. Metal barbecues and hibachis have the advantage of being portable: They can be moved fairly easily from deck to patio and taken along when it's time to move to a new home.

Obviously, plants must be kept away from the heat of the barbecue—high heat and green leaves are a fatal combination. When it's not in use, a brick or stone barbecue can function as a shelf for potted plants. These can decorate the table or the patio when the barbecue is being used.

Traditional barbecues and fireplaces may recall childhood and add to the charm of present-day family gatherings.

A portable grill allows an outdoor fireplace to double as a barbecue. Also, an outdoor fireplace can extend the season of outdoor living by making the area warmer on evenings that would otherwise be uncomfortably chilly. Some fireplaces are brick or stone like those indoors; others are sunken concrete fire pits; and others are circular metal bowls that can be moved wherever guests have gathered. Fireplaces and fire pits have the advantage of adding permanent value; portable fireplaces have the advantage of movability—you can place one wherever the view of the city lights is best or the shooting stars of August are the most dramatic. Like barbecues, outdoor fireplaces expand the usefulness of an outdoor room and significantly increase the real living space of a house or apartment by ensuring that the deck or patio or balcony is used often.

Plants trailing from the mantel and potted camellias used as a screen turn this unusable outdoor fireplace into a showplace.

Ties With Nature

The designer of a deck or patio environment has a unique asset: All of nature can be part of his or her palette. Selecting flowers, vines, shrubs, and trees that will attract birds and other wildlife can be a special pleasure.

Bird havens   In addition to the delight of seeing and hearing them, a gardener who encourages birds enjoys the substantial fringe benefit of having fewer insects on the deck and in the garden. Hummingbirds snatch insects in addition to feeding on nectar; many other birds eat grubs, bugs, and caterpillars. Fewer flies, gnats, and mosquitoes means a more comfortable deck for people; fewer aphids and other sucking, gnawing, leaf-stripping spoilers makes the outdoor room a better place for the garden and the gardener.

You can supply three of the things birds need to survive: water, shelter, and food. Supply water by providing a fountain, waterfall, pool, fish pond, or birdbath. To provide shelter, plant trees, shrubs, and vines or erect birdhouses. You can provide birds with food in two ways: by hanging bird feeders and by growing the plants birds feed on. The more of these elements that are available, the greater the number of birds that will frequent your outdoor room. In the fourth chapter, the section called Miniature Sanctuaries for Birds offers specific suggestions about feeders and plants that invite birds.

Butterfly gardens   To attract butterflies, consider planting bloodflower, blue mistbush, butterfly weed, or butterfly bush. Remember to include a water source. For more suggestions, see the section called The Butterfly Farm, in the fourth chapter.

Habitats for other wildlife   Sometimes an outdoor room is such an inviting habitat that its owner has more contact with nature than he or she bargained for. If your design includes a pool with fish, plan how to protect them from cats and raccoons. These mammals consider all fish, including your prized (and pricey) Japanese koi, to be on their menu. In addition, raccoons will cheerfully dig up waterlilies and other aquatic plants. In the fourth chapter, the section called Wondrous Water Gardens discusses how to install hardware cloth a few inches below the surface of the water. In place,

the wire is nearly invisible, and it does a fine job of protecting fish and foliage.

For most people, however, the problems caused by wildlife are few and are far outweighed by the pleasure the creatures bring. Most landscape designers, professionals and do-it-yourselfers, choose to encourage ties with nature by providing food and shelter. In fact, by doing so, you can make up for some of the loss of natural habitat. For example, the red berries of American holly supply winter food for more than 40 species of birds. If you really want to get involved in providing habitat, make a sketch of your yard or patio. Include labels identifying trees, bushes, vines, flowers, and water sources. Send the sketch and five dollars to the National Wildlife Federation Backyard Wildlife Habitat Program, 1412 Sixteenth Street NW, Washington, DC 20036. Federation staff will certify your yard as an official Backyard Wildlife Habitat if it contains sufficient food, water, and cover. If it doesn't, the federation will make suggestions so that your yard can attain certification.

EVALUATING PLANT SPECIES

Now that you have reviewed the major elements of the landscape designer's palette, you are ready to focus on the element that, in most cases, requires the most planning: the plants.

After you decide on the effect you want to achieve, many factors remain to be considered before you can choose specific plants to create that effect.

• The disadvantages of the plants
• All aspects of the climate
• The need for color throughout the year
• Vertical space
• How well the plant can adapt to life in a container

As you consider plant possibilities, you'll have an advantage over garden designers and houseplant gardeners: The range of plants for an outdoor room is larger than that for the garden or house. Why? Because pots are portable. Houseplants can be brought outside to create the look of lush greenery for the summer and be all the healthier for the experience. Bulbs can be overwintered in the basement or garage.

Left: A fountain not only draws birds, but the sound of water can mask the noise of traffic or neighbors' voices. Right: This waterfall fountain cascades into a pool, adding a woodland touch and the magic of falling water.

Top: Raking leaves seems a small price to pay for the dramatic dash of seasonal color provided by burning bush (Euonymus alata). *Bottom: The owner of this Oregon garden wanted the effect of a palm. The windmill palm is hardy to 10°F.*

Consider the Disadvantages

When you choose trees or flowers, consider the amount of raking and sweeping you are willing to do. Trees, shrubs, and flowers all drop things on the patio: leaves, flowers, seedpods, bark, and so on. You can spend a great deal of time cleaning up after eucalyptus trees, which drop everything—leaves, twigs, branches, blossoms, seeds, long strips of bark—incessantly. If the choice of what to plant is yours, consider putting in trees that aren't inherently untidy.

The scarlet leaves of a liquid amber may strike you as beautiful against the silver-gray of a weathered redwood deck, a picture of fall to be enjoyed in and of itself. Pale pink plum blossoms scattered on a herringbone brick patio may be the essence of spring for you. Blue jacaranda flowers on the stones of the courtyard and floating gracefully in the fountain may be a delight to the eye.

On the other hand, fallen hibiscus flowers on pavement are as slippery as banana peels. Spiny, spiky coast-live-oak (*Quercus agrifolia*) leaves are sharp to step on with bare feet. Peaches (*Prunus persica*) have an unpleasant propensity to plop—a fact that means not only a squishy mess but bees and wasps as well. Coconut palms (*Arecastrum romanzoffianum*) actually *do* drop coconuts from great heights, just like in the cartoons. This is one of the situations where an ounce of prevention is worth several pounds of cure: It's far easier not to plant a troublesome tree than to dig it up or cut it down.

Match the Plants to the Climate

A subtropical jungle will grow only if subtropical plants can survive outdoors both winter and summer. That's perfectly possible in parts of Florida, southern California, Puerto Rico, the Virgin Islands, and Hawaii, but a little tough to carry off in the rest of North America. In areas where the climate permits only summer use of the deck, courtyard, lanai, or patio, it may be wiser to think in terms of bulbs in spring, annuals for summer, and some sturdy evergreens that will keep the space looking alive even in the dead of winter. A simple scheme would be window boxes of giant crocuses for the earliest bloom, rectangular planters crammed with daffodils in spring, big pots of daisies or petunias that bloom all summer long, some chrysanthemums to welcome fall, and the glossy deep

Shrubs like camellias will winter nicely in unheated sunrooms, as will tender trees such as citrus—as long as the temperature doesn't drop below freezing. (Citrus provide an extra bonus when wintered indoors: They bloom in winter and the fragrance is wonderful.) Likewise, cool-weather orchids, such as cymbidiums and cattleyas, can flourish as the result of a seasonal move. Brought outdoors for the summer, they set bud; brought indoors for the winter, they bloom for months. In making your plant selection, don't overlook the possibility of summering plants—that is, putting them outdoors during the warm season. It's an excellent way to make an outdoor room look lush during the period that the space gets the most use.

The remainder of this section presents the points you should consider when evaluating plants for your outdoor room.

green leaves and red berries of holly bushes to brighten winter.

Temperature is not the only consideration in choosing plants. Sun, shade, wind, and rain all help determine which plants flourish; which look perpetually tatty; or, worse, which die. To determine the conditions your plants have to live with, play detective. In a handy garden notebook, jot down how many hours of sun or shade your outdoor room gets. Note day and night temperatures—a minimum-maximum thermometer works well for this as long as you remember to check it every day. A significant difference between day and night temperatures may determine when and how prolifically your plants bloom. For example, a 50° drop from 90° to 40°F is not at all unusual in desert areas in the summer; in the Midwest, however, there may be only a few degrees difference between the temperatures at noon and midnight.

When the deck gets sun is important. Flowers that thrive in morning sun may wilt or scald in direct midday sun; plants that love full sun at high noon may not bloom as profusely with only early morning or late afternoon light.

Prevailing wind patterns also make a difference in what will grow well. Some plants, like rhododendrons and Japanese maples (*Acer palmatum*), look thoroughly miserable when exposed to wind; others, like tall marigolds, are easily broken by it. A low-growing common geranium (*Pelargonium × hortorum*) is more likely to grow if there is no wind. The windier it is, the more plants need water, since wind strips both leaves and soil of moisture.

How much rain the space gets is important too. If it doesn't rain regularly, someone will have to water the plants. In the third chapter, the section called Planning How to Water discusses irrigation options.

If you live in an area with low rainfall, drought-resistant plants are the logical choice. That doesn't mean you are limited to using cactuses and succulents, however. A great many widely grown garden plants are semisucculent and capable of managing perfectly well without a lot of water. Garden geraniums, regal pelargoniums, ivy geraniums, and petunias are just a few examples. Bulbs also work well in the water-conservative garden. Bulbs store moisture, which helps tide them over when water is scarce. Crocuses, daffodils, narcissuses, and hyacinths all bloom early in the spring; in August, an amaryllis perfumes the patio with its pink flowers. A plant with fleshy roots, such as agapanthus, can also manage long periods

For a simple, old-fashioned effect, consider geraniums. They are easy to care for and seem to thrive on a certain amount of neglect.

without a lot of water. It's hard to feel deprived on a patio with planters ablaze with gloriosa daisy, bearded iris, red-hot-poker, red valerian, euryops, and blanket-flower—yet each and every one tolerates drought. In fact, they go beyond tolerating drought; they prefer it.

If your deck, patio, or porch accompanies a seaside cottage, you must take salt air and salt spray into consideration as well as the sea breezes. Lantana, *Rosa rugosa*, euryops, impatiens, nasturtium, lavender, and statice are all proven performers along seacoasts.

Consider Container Depth

Perhaps you have a container and are searching for a plant to fill it. Some plants are naturally shallow rooted: pansies, azaleas, and ferns, for instance. Others, such as cup-and-saucer campanula or parsley, are deep rooted. Shallow-rooted plants can languish in deep containers even when the soil at the bottom is still moist—their roots can't reach far enough to get the water they need. Deep-rooted plants may push themselves out of the soil if their roots hit the impenetrable bottom of a shallow pot. Make sure pots and plants are a good match for each other.

Siberian dogwood (Cornus alba 'Sibirica') has red bark that is striking in winter as well as attractive flowers in spring.

Provide Seasonal Color

A well-planned garden shows something of interest in every season, whether it is masses of summer flowers or a dramatic winter silhouette. Japanese maples (*Acer palmatum*), for example, are lovely in leaf, color well in autumn, and have an interesting silhouette in winter. Flowering cherry trees bloom flamboyantly in spring, offer shade in summer, and reveal dramatic bark texture in winter. Quite a few trees have strikingly beautiful bark colors or eye-catching bark texture. The Japanese maple *Acer palmatum* 'Sangokaku' has bright red bark; certain dogwoods (*Cornus*) have red or yellow bark; unusual birches (*Betula*) may have copper-colored or purple bark. Some bamboos (*Bambusa*), although not exactly trees (they are grasses, in fact), have handsome gleaming black or gold bark. Strong, clear colors are especially welcome against the dark gray of winter skies or the brilliant background of new snow. In the fourth chapter, in the section called Color for All Seasons, you will find sample designs for each time of year. Each design cites plants by species; perhaps you'll find the very species you need to provide the seasonal color you envision.

Consider Vertical Space

One way to get more plants into a small area is to make use of the vertical space. You can grow vines up walls, put trellises in pots, or grow trees and shrubs as espaliers. The use of vertical space leaves more level space for other uses, giving the feeling and the fact of more room. Plants can soften the look of house walls, garden walls, and fences. Plants in the vertical space can block unappealing views of children's swing sets, trash cans, or the alley behind the house. They can create a sense of privacy and make the view from within the outdoor room spectacular. A wall of Boston ivy or Virginia creeper is magnificent when it colors crimson in the fall. Espaliered apple trees are exquisite when their white blossoms herald spring. Pots or planters with tall trellises covered with trumpet vine (*Campsis radicans*) are lush with greenery and bright with yellow or orange flowers all summer long.

When you select plant species for your deck or patio, consider how vines and climbers, hanging and trailing plants, and plants on shelves can further the design you have chosen.

Vines and climbers Vines grown over arbors can provide cooling summer shade. Deciduous vines, when they lose their leaves, can open the outdoor room to winter sunshine. Vines can be grown for their foliage, their flowers, or their fragrance. Some, such as star-jasmine or climbing roses, offer all three. Star-jasmine (Confederate jasmine) is a richly fragrant climber; as it grows up a verandah wall or on a trellis near a window, its scent is the smell of long summer evenings. Climbing roses are splendid over arches, clambering up posts, sprawling along a wall or fence, or even climbing a tree. Sweet autumn clematis provides a profusion of flowers at a time when most of the summer show is over; prune this plant to the ground and it will come back vigorously with the spring. Any sunny balcony can be made magnificent with big pots of mixed morning glories climbing up green string or twined on a balcony railing. For summer days and nights of floriferous glory, try mixing fragrant night-blooming white moonflower (*Ipomoea alba*) with purple-flowered ivy-leafed morning glory (*I. hederacea*) or pale blue 'Heavenly Blue' morning glory (*I. tricolor*). Give a partially shaded stucco or masonry wall a delicate tracery with the dainty white-margined creeping fig (*Ficus pumila* 'Variegatas').

Plants that hang Baskets, brackets, and window boxes can be the means of enhancing vertical space by suspending plants from the eaves, walls, sills, or railings. Hanging baskets create the ambience of a bower. Hung from the eaves in front of a window, a hanging basket of flowers can improve the view immediately. Used on a small apartment balcony, hanging baskets allow you to garden in the air, saving precious floor space for furniture. Hung from the ceiling of a sun porch or verandah, baskets brighten the view from both inside and out.

There are a great many plants that drape or trail attractively. Some have handsome foliage; others have colorful flowers; and some, such as the spider plant (*Chlorophytum comosum*), simply have a curious growth habit. A spider plant grows new little plants on its long, arching flower stems. Its common name in Spanish is *mala madre,* meaning bad mother, because it "throws" its babies out. Basket-of-gold forms big round balls of blossoms. 'Basket King' or 'Sweet 100' tomato plants are both beautiful and edible.

Wall-mounted plants There are a variety of ways to hang pots on walls—wrought-iron brackets into which traditional terra-cotta pots

Left: Boston ivy (Parthenocissus tricuspidata) transforms a stone or brick wall into an attractive living screen.
Right: Hanging plants on a balcony or patio can screen an ugly view.

Used as cachepots for annuals or permanent planters for perennials, window boxes can provide a delightful venue for the space-limited gardener. Be sure the boxes are securely attached to ledges or sills.

may be slipped, for example. In southern Spain such pots are typically planted with crayon-red geraniums. Pots can be taken out of the wrought-iron brackets for easy watering, if you object to water running down the side of the house. Large molded terra-cotta planters are too heavy to take down to water, so plan to hang them where draining water won't stain the wall.

Plants for window boxes   For a bright spring and summer window-box display, especially in cold climates, plant annuals because they bloom the longest. Warm-climate window boxes can feature perennials such as pelargoniums, primroses, or asparagus ferns. Trailing plants are especially effective in window boxes. English ivies (particularly the variegated varieties), vining nasturtiums, and star-jasmines can cascade gracefully over the sides of a box until it is completely covered. Bulbs can be planted under vines so their flowers peek through each year to welcome spring. The biggest disadvantage to window boxes with annual plantings is that there is no winter display in cold regions. The disadvantage of perennial plantings is that they inevitably go through periods when the plants are out of bloom, or need trimming, or have just been trimmed. At these times the boxes are not looking their best.

Using the window box as a sort of cachepot for pots of flowers at the peak of flamboyant bloom solves the problem of the window box not always being in display condition. As one set of flowers begins to be past bloom, replace it with the next set of seasonal performers. Use dwarf conifers or small hollies in winter, daffodils or fairy primroses in spring, daisies or petunias in summer, and Michaelmas daisies or chrysanthemums in autumn. The disadvantage to the cachepot approach is that it can seem more like flower arranging than gardening. The pleasure of watching seeds sprout or the first bud open may not be there, but since the pleasure of seeing flowers blooming and bright certainly is, a cachepot window box is worth considering. It may fit the way you live better than planting and tending.

The urban farmer can sow a summer-salad window box with miniature vegetable plants such as 'Pixie Hybrid II' or 'Tiny Tim' tomato, 'Butterball' carrot, and 'Tom Thumb' lettuce. The serious cook might want to grow herbs in a window box under the kitchen window. Oregano, sweet marjoram, sweet basil, parsley, cilantro, chives, shallots, summer savory, a variety of sages, and a multiplicity of thymes can all do well in a window box.

A shaded window box can hold a combination of small woodland ferns and pansies; a sunny summer one might have dwarf Unwin dahlias, dwarf Transvaal daisies, French marigolds, or 'Peter Pan' zinnias. A sophisticated and maintenance-free window box might hold a collection of trailing English ivies: perhaps a solid green 'Fluffy Ruffles', a green and gold 'Gold Dust', and a green and white 'Baltica'. The last of these is not only hardy, but it turns purple with cold. To have the trailing effect of ivy and flowers, try ivy geranium (*Pelargonium peltatum*) or 'Cascade' petunias. A window box filled with scarlet sage is bright in its own right and attracts hummingbirds as well. The city soul who longs for a proper English country garden can even grow semi-dwarf 'Fantasia' delphiniums, 27 inches high with 15-inch flower spikes. (These are much easier to manage in a window box than 'Pacific Giant', which grows to 5 feet tall.)

Perhaps the view out the window is objectionable. Fasten strings from the window box to the top of the window and grow sweet peas or scarlet runner beans up the string. Sweet peas will perfume the room from outside the window. Because they must be picked regularly to keep them blooming, there will be flowers in bouquets about the house as well. Outside a child's window, fasten strings and plant scarlet runner beans. After the fire-engine red flowers drop, the child can pick fresh beans right from the sill.

A variation on the theme of window boxes is the French balcony planter frame, a sort of rectangular basket-cum-hooks. The frame hangs over a balcony railing and holds pots. Like hanging baskets and trellised vines, planter frames provide the beauty of flowers without taking up precious floor space.

Plants for shelves   Étagères fleurs, tiered metal shelves, are another way of using vertical space. Such shelves are available in a wide variety of sizes and shapes, from quarter rounds that tuck neatly into a corner to simple rectangles. Most are less than 2 feet wide, ample to hold lots of pots without taking up half the patio. They are especially effective for displaying collections: a variety of succulents or miniature roses or spring bulbs or oriental lilies or chrysanthemums.

The urban farmer might consider using étagères to grow such space-saving vegetables as bush snap beans, bush lima beans, bush

shell beans, bush squashes, bush cantaloupe, bush cucumbers (for eating raw, or pickling, or both), 'Pixie Hybrid II' tomatoes, spinach, red or green chard, radishes, scallions, a variety of chili peppers, and even a bush 'Sugar Baby' watermelon for summer desserts. The gourmet gardener could use an étagère to grow a proper mixture of gourmet lettuces (Ruby, Royal Oak Leaf, Black-seeded Simpson, Merveille de Quatre Saisons, and Green Curled Endive, for starters), radicchio, 'Tiny Tim' cherry tomatoes, 'Little Finger' baby carrots, bush green beans, 'Petit Provençal' peas, and certainly some shallots and garlic. A collection of fresh herbs of every possible sort can put an étagère to a pretty and practical use. You can use the herbs for cooking; for teas and tisanes; for potpourri; for perfuming linens with lavender; and even, in the case of tansy and wormwood, for insect and moth repellent.

The addition of the exotic potted pineapple in the background turns a patch of ordinary herbs and vegetables into a miniature jungle.

Consider Trees

Trees for patios must meet special criteria: They need to be fairly small and comparatively slow-growing. Trees can do so many delightful things that there is a terrible temptation to try to find the one that can do everything—flower in the spring, bear delicious fruit in the summer, color magnificently in the fall, and remain green through the winter. The typical homeowner wants a tree superbly adapted to the climate, but so unusual that no one else in the neighborhood has one like it. And, of course, the tree must be useful—earning, so to speak, its horticultural keep. In summer heat, it should shade and cool; in winter chill, it should let in precious sunshine. How are you to choose?

The place to begin, once again, is with your own needs. Decide whether the patio needs shade or if shade will make it chilly and uncomfortable. Will the tree eventually block the view? If you live in a city, the tree must tolerate the air pollution. Can the tree live 25 years in a pot or only 5? Will the tree be a windbreak or will it need a windbreak? Will it bring birds to feed? Will you be able to eat, can, preserve, or give away all the fruit? If you are renting, the tree should be able to go with you when you move. If there are toddlers about, no part of the tree should be poisonous.

It's worth thinking about the angle from which the tree will be viewed. Will you be looking up into it from a patio, down on it from a balcony, or directly at it from eye level? Dwarf citrus, for example, are especially rewarding at eye level. They provide shiny, green leaves the year around, sweetly fragrant flowers right at your nose, and fruit you can pick without a ladder. *Magnolia soulangiana* is superb to look down upon, since most of its large, delicately shaded flowers are at the top of the tree. A mayten, which is like a willow with good manners, is extremely pleasant to lounge under while looking up into its green leaves and graceful branches.

A potted ficus tree (Ficus benjamina) helps bring the outdoors inside in this indoor-outdoor sunporch.

When selecting trees for your deck or patio, you have two categories of choices: trees in pots and freestanding trees.

Trees in pots A pot containing a tree can give a double show when the tree is underplanted with flowers. Summer annuals, with their profuse bloom and long flowering period, are especially effective in this role. Yellow French marigolds, purple sweet alyssum, dark blue lobelia, gaily striped red-and-white petunias—any one of these would add an extra spot of color planted under a potted tree. Trailing plants, such as miniature ivies or yellow archangels, look handsome cascading over the sides of the box or pot. Ground covers such as dichondra or baby's tears have a cool, quiet look that sets trees off well. Underplantings of carrots or curled parsley give the impression that the tree is growing amidst ferns and have the added advantage of being edible.

Even the smallest deck or balcony can accommodate a collection of trees in the form of bonsai. Though bonsai provide no shade, they can certainly provide a few flowers in spring; a spot of green in summer; and color in fall, depending on the species. Japanese black pine, Japanese maple, and flowering cherry trees are traditional bonsai choices, but any intriguingly shaped tree is a potential candidate for a bonsai pot. Because the purpose of bonsai is to suggest an entire landscape in a minuscule space, a bonsai tree is especially valuable where room is at a premium. A twisted tree, a rock, and a scrap of moss may be all that's needed to call to mind a windswept mountain ridge. The chapter of sample designs, "Selecting Your Scene," includes a bonsai garden that you may be able to use as a source of inspiration for your own design.

Freestanding trees Not all patio trees must be grown in pots. Garden space next to a patio can be used to plant a tree that will shade the patio, or bricks can be removed to make space in which to plant a tree. In these cases, you must find out if the roots will lift the paving or crack the concrete, as sycamore roots can. Roots may also wreak havoc with the lawn or garden, as the roots of Siberian elms often do, or invade water lines, a nasty habit for which weeping willows and poplars are notorious.

In addition to being decorations in themselves, the trunks and branches of existing trees can be pressed into service to support decorations. Baskets of hanging ferns or flowers can be suspended from the branches. In tropical and subtropical climates, bark slabs with orchids, bromeliads, and staghorn ferns can be spectacular fastened to trunks. If there are trees near enough to the patio, you can hang a hammock. If a nearby tree is sturdy enough, hang an old-fashioned wooden lovers' swing or a baby's swing.

If a deck is built around an existing tree, keep in mind that the hole must accommodate the girth of the tree at maturity, not just the current size. A circular or half-circle bench around the trunk can provide extra seating in the shade, or it may take up far too much space. The tree can be the focus of the deck or merely contribute to its shade and comfort. Make sure any decorative accoutrements, such as a bird feeder or baskets of fuchsias, don't become things on which to whack your head.

After you have made a list of appropriate plants, your next steps are to prepare the outdoor room for their purchase and arrival.

The small, well-behaved shadbush tree (Amelanchier canadensis)—*also called serviceberry, juneberry, and shad-blow—may be the near-perfect patio tree. It has attractive early-spring flowers, summer berries, superb fall colors, and attractive silver bark.*

Preparing for Plants

You have decided how you want to use your outdoor room, and you have determined the kind of plants and furnishings it needs. You may feel ready for action, but a few planning steps remain.

Now that you have a general idea of what you want, you must fill in the details. For the plants, what containers will be most appropriate? How will you feed and water the plants? How will you protect them from insects, neighborhood pests, and disease? If you will be gardening on a balcony or rooftop, how can you be sure that the structure can support the weight of the furnishings? How can you hang planters safely, and how can you ensure that a planter, once filled, will be movable? In addition to helping you establish the fine points of your design, this chapter will tell you how to select healthy plants when you go to the nursery or garden center.

This arresting composition of dusty miller (Senecia cineraria) *and* Lobelia *'Crystal Palace' is a focal point on the deck.*

The oriental flavor of this secluded nook is created by a pot, the shape of the rhododendron, and the ornamental stone.

CHOOSING CONTAINERS

A container can be anything that will hold soil. Container drainage is usually a prerequisite for healthy plants. In some cases, however, as with tin-lined window boxes, a container does not even have to drain. Some containers, such as bonsai pots, are for specific purposes; others, such as azalea or bulb pans, are for specific plants. Some pots are formal—Versailles tubs or Italian stone urns, for example. Others are so simple and familiar that they seem homey and cozy—consider the classic clay flowerpot.

Pots

As unique as a one-of-a-kind piece hand-thrown by a master potter or as convenient as a plastic six-pack tray, pots come in a tremendous variety of shapes and sizes.

Terra-cotta pots   Because they are porous, terra-cotta pots "breathe"—this allows essential oxygen to get to plant roots. However, that same porosity means that terra-cotta pots dry out faster than glazed or plastic pots.

Painted and glazed pots   Handsome designs, such as the exquisitely pale handpainted peonies on a Chinese pot, may attract you to one container. Beautiful glazing may draw you to another. Because a glaze prevents moisture from evaporating through the sides of the pot, glazed pots hold moisture longer than clay pots. This is excellent, so long as water is not applied with a heavy hand. Watered too frequently, plants in glazed pots can easily die.

Plastic pots   Plastic nursery pots have so many excellent, practical qualities that it seems unfair to fault them on their appearance. They are lightweight; they retain moisture well; they tolerate both heat and cold; they are inexpensive; they last; they are unbreakable; they stack and store conveniently; they are far easier to work with than the metal cans they replaced; and, if you drop an empty one on your toe, you probably won't even say *ouch.* Keep in mind that you can overcome the appearance of a plastic pot by slipping it into a cachepot or handsome basket.

Plastic pots do have a few drawbacks besides their appearance. Plastic does not last a long time if exposed to sun; ultraviolet rays make it brittle and susceptible to cracking. Colored plastics tend to fade in strong sunlight. The fact that plastic pots retain moisture well makes it easy to overwater plants that live in them. Still, these are small problems compared to all their useful qualities.

Window Boxes

If your container of choice is the window box, consider these two ways to use it: filled with soil and planted with flowers or filled with pots of flowers already in bloom. Each method has its own advantages. Planting directly into soil seems more like gardening. It's a chance to get dirt under your nails, feel the soil, and watch seeds or seedlings grow and bud and bloom. For the perpetually urban, it may be as close to real gardening as it's possible to get in the city.

Planters and Tubs

The material a planter or tub is made of determines its characteristics.

Wooden planters   Redwood or cedar planters weather to a handsome silvery gray. They require no maintenance whatsoever, and they

The humblest flowers can be set off by a whimsical window box.

last for many years. When their cost is amortized over the years of their usefulness, their expense often seems justified. Plants grow well in wooden planters because they usually have excellent drainage. Painted wooden planters have an attractive crisp look. They do require some maintenance, usually a fresh coat of paint every few years, to keep them looking their best. Spanking-white Versailles tubs show off specimen trees and topiary to splendid advantage.

Fiberglass planters Versailles tubs are also available in fiberglass. They last a long time, endure all kinds of weather, don't require repainting, and are not nearly as heavy as wood. They tend to hold moisture well, since little is lost to evaporation.

Cast-iron planters Planters made of cast iron or lead are often beautiful, but they are extremely heavy. They last forever—as long as they are not cracked by a sharp blow or by being dropped. Cast iron does have a tendency to rust, which means it may need a regular spring session with the spray paint to keep it looking handsome. Keep in mind that rust can stain concrete patios or wooden decks. Lead, unlike cast iron, acquires a magnificent patina and grows ever more beautiful. Both of these materials can be superb additions to an outdoor room.

Ornate planters require plants that neither dwarf them nor distract the eye from their sculptural qualities.

"Found" Containers

You can use almost anything for a planter—from a weathered wheelbarrow to a clawfoot tub. Plants have been known to grow happily in all of them. Planters such as wheelbarrows and clawfoot tubs fall into the category of "found" containers. These are things that someone realized would make interesting planters although they were originally intended for purposes other than gardening.

Some found containers have proved to be such excellent planters that they have become classics themselves.

Half-barrels Not only are half-barrels superb planters, once the bottoms have been drilled with four or five drain holes, but they are big enough to accommodate trees, large shrubs, or a mini-garden of herbs or flowers. Also, they are inexpensive. If you live near wine country, you may be able to pick up wine barrels free for the hauling. If you don't, many garden centers offer them seasonally for very reasonable prices, considering their size. They require no maintenance, they last for years, and they develop more character as the seasons go by.

Chinese egg jars With their wonderful swirling dragons, Chinese egg jars are no longer inexpensive (antique dealers have discovered them). If there is a Chinese community nearby, however, you may be able to get the jars at a reasonable price directly from the Chinese grocery stores that sell preserved eggs. The jars are deep enough to grow small trees in: Imagine a pair of neatly trimmed bays (*Laurus nobilis*) or privets (*Ligustrum japonicum*) framing the front door. Egg jars look terrific with large shrubs like camellias and work wonderfully with morning-glory vines, which might well twine over French doors to a patio. Egg jars must be drilled for drainage, but they require no maintenance and they last for years. Dropped or bumped hard, Chinese egg jars can crack or chip. When filled with soil, they are very heavy, so, like half-barrels, they should be planted where they are going to stay.

Packing crates If you live near a seaport or airport, find out where the freight comes in and ask if extra crates are available. These sturdy wooden boxes are often quite large and often marked with intriguing foreign writing. Even if they say nothing more than "This end up" or "Fragile—Handle with care," they may look wonderfully exotic. To make packing boxes and shipping crates last longer, drill holes in the bottoms and line them with the heaviest plastic you can find. Slit the plastic over the holes to allow drainage. Shipping crates don't last as long as half-barrels or Chinese egg jars, but they will provide several years of service.

Unless you are aiming for a formal look, you can't go wrong with barrel planters. They stand the wear and tear of any weather and any location.

PROVIDING SOIL DRAINAGE AND NUTRIENTS

The kind of soil mix in the pot affects how well it retains moisture. Soils with lots of organic material, such as compost, absorb water easily and retain moisture well. Soils with a high proportion of sand, sharp gravel, or redwood bark tend to drain very quickly. Ordinarily, such soils are used for specialty plants: sand for cactuses and succulents, sharp gravel for alpine plants, and chunks of redwood bark for orchids. These materials are used to prevent excessive moisture from accumulating and rotting the roots; the plants used with the materials do best without too much water.

You are lucky if you have sandy loam in your garden that you can dig up and use for potting plants; most gardeners don't. It is, however, possible to purchase the ingredients and mix your own loamy soil. Use one part loam, one part compost, and one part clean sand. Most people simply buy packaged potting soil at the nursery or garden center. Most commercial potting mixes are adequate straight out of the bag.

If you prefer to do more than pour packaged soil into a pot, consider amending commercial soil to suit your plants. Rhododendrons, azaleas, and Japanese maples prefer an acidic soil, so you might add a little ground or shredded peat moss. Bulbs do better when a bit of bonemeal, a natural source of phosphorus, is added. Maidenhair ferns need to be kept constantly moist, so mix in some extra organic material, such as compost. Aquarium charcoal, available wherever tropical fish are sold, helps keep soil sweet. *Sweet* is the horticultural term for the absence of water molds that rot roots. (Soil that contains these molds is called sour.) Therefore, a little aquarium charcoal can be useful in pots with poor drainage and window boxes with steel, tin, or plastic liners. Don't forget to put a shard of clay or a piece of fine mesh screen over the drainage hole, to keep the soil in the pot.

Soil Nutrients

Ordinarily, plants absorb nutrients from the soil, through their roots. Plants grown in the ground can expand their roots into fresh soil when they have exhausted the nutrients in the immediate area. Potted plants cannot extend their roots beyond the pot, so it is important to feed and fertilize potted plants after they have absorbed the nutrients in the original potting soil.

The most important nutrients for plant growth are nitrogen, phosphorus, and potassium. All commercial plant foods contain these three elements. The proportion, or percentage, of each is listed on the label, in the order cited above. Plant foods and fertilizers are often described in terms of these percentages. For example, the nursery staff may tell you that your plants need a "10-10-10." That means the fertilizer should contain equal proportions of each nutrient, and each represents 10 percent of total ingredients. The active ingredients make up 30 percent of a plant food; the remaining 70 percent is a distributing agent that applies the fertilizer evenly.

Nitrogen in soil comes from the natural breakdown of once-living organisms. Nitrogen promotes healthy leaves and sturdy new stems. Compost is an excellent source of nitrogen. Phosphorus helps plants develop strong roots and grow steadily; without it, plants grow slowly and flowers don't develop properly. It stimulates flowering and the setting of fruit. Potassium wards off disease, stabilizes growth, and intensifies leaf and flower color. It is also called potash.

In addition to nitrogen, phosphorus, and potassium, certain trace elements are essential to plant health: boron, calcium, sulfur, magnesium, and iron. Some commercial fertilizers include them in their formulas; if you use compost in your soil mixture or add compost to packaged potting soils, you can usually provide sufficient quantities of trace elements to grow sturdy, healthy plants.

Fertilizers

It's true that potted plants do better with feeding, but there are a number of cautions. Most plants from nurseries and commercial growers have been heavily fertilized to bring them to marketable size quickly. Your new acquisitions don't need additional fertilizer. Likewise, newly repotted plants have been disturbed by the process of transplanting; they don't need feeding. Don't feed plants that are showing evidence of stress—wilting, leaf drop, or disease, for example. In short, remember this rule: Never feed a sick plant. The exception to the rule involves plants with yellowed leaves. Yellowed leaves can be caused by insufficient nitrogen. Unfortunately, they can also be caused by too much water or various plant ills. Ask the

Transplanting Nursery Plants

Make sure your nursery plants don't dry out while waiting to be transplanted

Use a flat-bladed knife, such as a putty knife, to cut through the soils and roots of plants in trays

Don't pull plants out of containers. Make sure the soil is moist but not wet. Tip the plant and let it fall gently into your hand.

Biodegradable containers require special handling. Punch holes in the bottom of a peat pot and cut off the upper edge until it is level with the soil in the pot. Rootballs dry out quickly if any part of the peat pot remains exposed, so plant below the soil line.

Set the plant into the soil at the level it grew before transplanting

Correct   Too low   Too high

Prune the roots of pot-bound plants by making three or four cuts from top to bottom down the side of the rootball; use a sharp knife

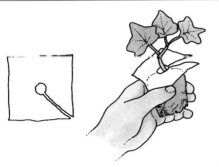

To plant a hanging basket, cut a 3-inch square of plastic film for each plant that will be placed in a hole in the side. Make a cut from one corner to the center. The plastic should slip around the stem of the plant.

After putting the plants through, put the plastic square around the stem on the outside of the pot. Tuck the plastic through the holes. This keeps soil from spilling out. Sphagnum moss packed around the stem and tucked into the hole prevents soil erosion.

Fill the container with soil, add remaining plants, and water thoroughly

If transplanting a plant wrapped in burlap, be sure to cut off the edge of the wrapping so it is below the soil surface

local agricultural extension agent before you feed a plant with yellowed leaves. (Extension agents are listed in the "Government" section of the telephone book, under "United States Department of Agriculture Extension Service" or under the subheading "Cooperative Extension Service," which appears under the heading for the state university. Some counties also have cooperative extension services.)

The best fertilizers for potted plants are water-soluble plant foods and liquid fertilizers, both of which are mixed with water before application. They are easy to use, and the nutrients they contain are available immediately. For large perennial plants or shrubs, use slow-release fertilizers, little round pellets that release small amounts of fertilizer each time the plant is watered.

With fertilizer, if the manufacturer's recommended amount is good, half as much is better. Good gardeners apply half-strength solutions twice as often to avoid fertilizer salt buildup, damaged roots, and leaf burn. A white film or encrustation on clay pots is the clue that a plant has been overfertilized. Leach the soil with lots of water, scrub the outside of the pot clean, and put the plant on a diet for a while. Few potted plants need fertilizer more than once a month; for most, twice a year is sufficient. Feed flowering plants in the early spring to encourage bloom and new growth. Feed perennials again after blooming.

Foliar feeding For the most part, plants absorb nutrients from the soil, through their roots. They can also absorb nutrients through their leaves—this accounts for the fact that trees and shrubs look greener after a rain. It's not an optical illusion or solely attributable to the dust having been rinsed away: The nitrogen in the rain does make the leaves greener. Foliar feeding operates on the same principle, and it's easy to do if you use a watering can. Mix the solution according to the instructions on the label, and wet the leaves on both sides as you water. Watering cans come with roses, or perforated nozzles, of various sizes. The rose determines how fine or heavy the spray is. For foliar feeding, use a rose that keeps the solution from pouring out with such force that it damages the plant. Liquid fertilizers with a 1-2-1 ratio are most effective, so look for commercial fertilizers marked "5-10-5" or "10-20-10."

PLANNING HOW TO WATER

Water conservation is a major issue in many regions of the country, but it is essential to plan the method you are going to use to supply water no matter where you live. Decide this *before* you need to water.

Watering Methods

Let your needs, budget, facilities, and temperament determine if you will have a manual or automatic watering system.

Manual watering On a small balcony, a watering can may well be the simplest solution. On a large terrace, however, a few trips from the faucet with a heavy watering can will quickly persuade you that there must be a better way.

Where an outdoor spigot is handy, a garden hose and an effective nozzle may do. The key is having a nozzle or watering wand that delivers a gentle spray to rinse leaves, without breaking flower stems or washing half the soil out of the pot. Overhead watering with a hose is best done in the morning so that leaves can dry before evening. Fungus diseases, such as mildew, thrive when leaves are damp overnight.

One effective method of watering the plants in hanging baskets is to immerse the baskets one at a time in a bucket or tub of water until the soil in each basket is saturated. (This is also an easy way to fertilize hanging baskets.) The time-honored way to tell when the soil is sufficiently soaked is to check to see that it is no longer bubbling. When the bubbling has stopped, all the air spaces in the soil are filled with water, and the soil is properly saturated. Set the basket on a perforated plastic flat laid over the bucket and let excess water drain back into the bucket. This method reduces the drip factor substantially, as well as the weight: Water weighs 8 pounds per gallon, and there's no point in hoisting heavy things over your head if you don't have to. Besides, letting the pots drain back into the bucket will also conserve water.

Automatic watering Watering by hand can be a soul-satisfying pleasure, an opportunity to observe the trees and flowers closely, to rejoice in each unfurling leaf and opening bud. It can also be one more chore on a to-do list that is already far too long. If watering is the way you achieve a state of serene contentment, by all means, water by hand. If the plants risk dying of thirst every time the family goes to the mountains for the weekend, seriously consider an automatic watering system.

A drip irrigation system can conserve water and time, delivering water directly to the soil at a rate at which it can be fully absorbed. Made of modular flexible plastic tubing, such a system is comparatively inexpensive and reasonably easy to modify to serve pots, planters, window boxes, and even hanging baskets. Drip irrigation systems create less mess than traditional watering, and this fact may contribute to the mental well-being of the gardener: No water splashes on the patio or drips off the balcony, and no mud dribbles into the courtyard, waiting to be tracked into the house.

Drip irrigation systems can include timers to water automatically. For people who have tight schedules, travel frequently, or are trying to maintain potted plants at a weekend cottage, an automatic watering system can mean the difference between a summer of bright bloom and a deckful of sadly wilted plants.

Watering Frequency

To test soil for moisture, poke your index finger into the soil up to the first joint. If the soil is dry, water the plants; if it's moist, let it be.

Small pots dry out faster than large ones. Also, a large one is easier to water. During a heat wave, container plants may need daily watering and hanging baskets may need watering twice a day. Ordinarily, twice a week or less will do. The only way to be certain about what needs watering is to spend some time on the patio or deck every morning or evening, making sure nothing has wilted or is about to. With a big pitcher of cold lemonade close by and a tall glass in your hand, this could be the most pleasant time of the entire day.

Remember that all areas of the balcony, terrace, lanai, or deck may not get the same amount of sun. There may be corners that get early morning sun only. A window box on the north side of the house may be in shade most of the day. Another spot may bear the brunt of midday sun. Potted plants in shady places will probably need less water than pots that get sun most of the day; pots that are in sun all day are likely to need more.

Watering Tips

Wick

Inverted saucer

Extensions are handy for watering hanging plants and those in other hard-to-reach places

Waterproofed box

Wicks

Rain gutter

A wick, with one end in soil and the other in a container of water, may be unsightly, but it can serve admirably when you are away on vacation

Gutter with holes

Watering large numbers of potted plants is easier with a gutter

Water-Efficient Irrigation

Drought occurs periodically in various parts of the nation. Finding ways to use water efficiently during these periods is essential. Avoid watering areas that have no plants. Make sure plants are not so pot bound that there's hardly any soil left to absorb and retain moisture. A third alternative is to choose plants that are naturally drought resistant.

PREVENTING INSECTS, PESTS, AND DISEASES

Most decks and patio plantings are small enough that insects, pests, and diseases rarely present major problems. Nevertheless, forewarned is forearmed.

Insect Prevention

The best preventive against garden pests is healthy plants. Plants that have all the water and nutrients they need are not immune, but they *are* more resistant to disease and insect damage. An annual autumn cleanup to clear the area of dead leaves, pruned vines, trimmed branches, and other miscellany prevents insects and disease organisms from overwintering in ground debris. Heap garden waste on the compost pile, or put it in closed leaf bags to be hauled away. Some municipal ordinances prohibit putting garden refuse in regularly scheduled trash pickups. Check with your local authorities to find out what you should do with garden waste.

When pests damage container gardens, slugs, snails, and earwigs are the likely culprits. From the amount of damage they can do, it seems they must eat all night. They all like to hide in dark, cool, moist places during the day. Check under pots in the morning and dispose of the creatures you find. Pests such as caterpillars and cutworms can be picked off and dealt with summarily. Other pests, such as aphids and mealybugs, can be washed off with a hard spray from the hose. These are the natural methods of dealing with garden pests.

The organic methods of insect prevention are general-purpose sprays based on rotenone or pyrethrum, and insecticidal soaps. Stronger measures, in the form of longer-lasting, more powerful chemical sprays, include diazinon, Sevin®, malathion, and Orthene®. These preventives are the most common insect sprays sold at nurseries and garden centers or the active ingredients in such sprays. Apply insecticides mixed with water to the soil to control aphids, thrips, leafminers, mealybugs, and insects that cause scale. Slugs and snails are best controlled with snail bait.

Measures Against Other Marauders

Some garden pests do not lend themselves to sweeping, stomping, or spraying: deer, rabbits, and other marauders. The pest list may include the neighbor's cat, who loves to dig in the soil of freshly potted plants. The best solution, chicken-wire cages around the plants, isn't very attractive, but it is effective. A tall fence around the yard may help discourage deer. A large dog or cat on the patio may discourage rabbits. Nothing discourages cats.

Disease Prevention

The first line of defense against plant diseases caused by bacteria, molds, and viruses are disease-resistant cultivars. The second is a tidy garden. The fall-back position is a commercial spray specifically developed to control that particular disease on that particular plant. Trimming off affected leaves and stems helps prevent diseases from spreading. Move diseased plants away from the healthy plants and isolate them until they are either treated or discarded. To determine what, exactly, your plant has, put an affected leaf in a plastic bag and take it to a local nursery or extension agent for diagnosis.

If a plant must be discarded, sterilize its pot before reusing it. You can sterilize clay or ceramic pots by washing them in the dishwasher or scrubbing them and pouring boiling water over them. A third method is to make a mild bleach solution (1 cup bleach to 1 gallon water), pour it over the pot, and then hose the pot down thoroughly to rinse away all trace of the bleach.

CONSIDERING LIVE LOAD

The term *live load* refers to the things put on a deck or balcony: the people, furniture, pots, and so on. If you garden on a balcony or rooftop, you must consider the weight of the live load and ensure that the structure can support it. If you don't, you could end up with cracks in the roofing, leaks in the ceiling, or worse.

Estimate the weight of the live load before you begin investing in your outdoor room.

Wherever you garden, make sure dripping water will not cause problems. Landlords and neighbors do not appreciate waterlogged walls, floors, or ceilings. Here, irrigation problems are minimized by using succulents, which don't need to be drenched.

Remember to consider the weight of water in garden ponds you create in containers. (The formulas for determining water volume and weight are in the fourth chapter, in the section called Wondrous Water Gardens.) If you live in an apartment building, ask the owner or manager if the structure can support the weight and get written permission before beginning construction. In a condominium, consult the homeowners' association. Homeowners can ask a local contractor whether cantilevered decks can adequately support the proposed plantings, furnishings, and decorations.

In addition, ask the local building department before you begin construction. In some areas rooftop gardening is prohibited.

PREVENTING LEAKS AND DRIPS

The neighbors of balcony gardeners may applaud the charm and beauty of the flowers, but they are likely to be less enthusiastic about water that drips or mud that trickles onto their balconies. Fortunately, there are lots of ways to control dripping water. The simplest is to catch overflow in waterproof saucers of sufficient depth and diameter. Glazed ceramic saucers and plastic saucers are waterproof. Terra-cotta saucers, being porous, tend to absorb water and may leave circular water stains on wooden decks. Inexpensive, lightweight clear plastic liners can be put inside clay saucers to prevent them from absorbing water or inside baskets to

Fastening Hangers to Walls and Ceilings

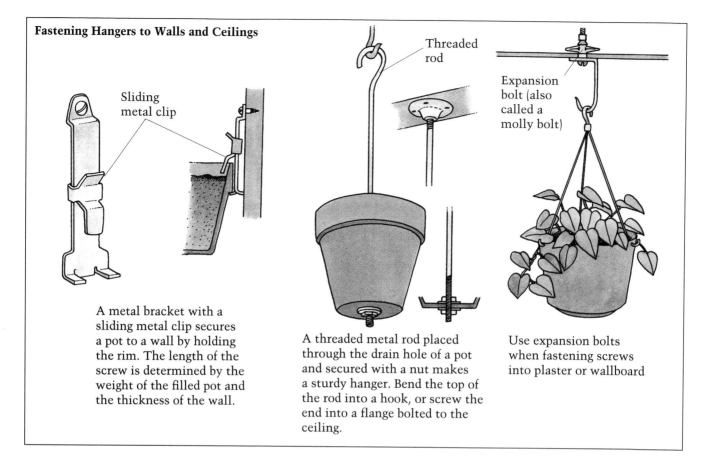

A metal bracket with a sliding metal clip secures a pot to a wall by holding the rim. The length of the screw is determined by the weight of the filled pot and the thickness of the wall.

A threaded metal rod placed through the drain hole of a pot and secured with a nut makes a sturdy hanger. Bend the top of the rod into a hook, or screw the end into a flange bolted to the ceiling.

Use expansion bolts when fastening screws into plaster or wallboard

keep the bottoms dry. Be sure to put waterproof saucers under wall-hung pots and pots that hang from balcony railings.

If you are gardening on a rooftop, remember to make sure that the roof is watertight. Protect the roofing material from constant foot traffic by installing duckboard or some other kind of wooden decking. See that waterproofing, such as PVC plastic, is under every container. Make sure that water is directed only to the plants; it must not drip or spray onto the roof.

SUSPENDING PLANTERS SAFELY

Hanging baskets present a few special requirements by virtue of the fact that they are suspended in air. Their hooks must be securely fastened so containers don't come tumbling down. Eye hooks screwed into wooden beams should be at least ½ inch long. Hooks screwed into plaster or wallboard should be supported with expansion bolts. Wrought-iron hangers that attach to stucco or wooden walls need screws long enough to hold them securely in place. The thickness of the pot wall and the weight when the pot is filled will determine the length of the screws. Check with your local hardware store

for help. Choose strong, sturdy branches, if you are going to hang baskets from tree limbs, and make sure those limbs are out of the way of the wind. To hang baskets at exactly the height desired, lengths of chain are very useful. Also useful are the slim, straight wires with hooks at either end. One hook is for attaching to the ceiling hook; the other is to hold the basket. These wires are available at nurseries.

PLANNING FOR PLANTER RELOCATION

Certainly, there are aesthetic considerations in choosing the style of the pots to go in your outdoor room. There are practical considerations as well. A large concrete basket-weave pot may look wonderful, but it is also extremely heavy. Add soil and water, and it is so heavy that it might as well be regarded as immovable. A plant that needs to be moved from one side of the deck to the other to take advantage of the shifting patterns of sunlight should have a container less likely to throw out your back. Alternatively, place the pot on a sturdy trolley with heavy-duty casters so it can be rolled from place to place.

Commercially manufactured plant trolleys are made of sturdy clear plastic or redwood.

Moving Heavy Plants

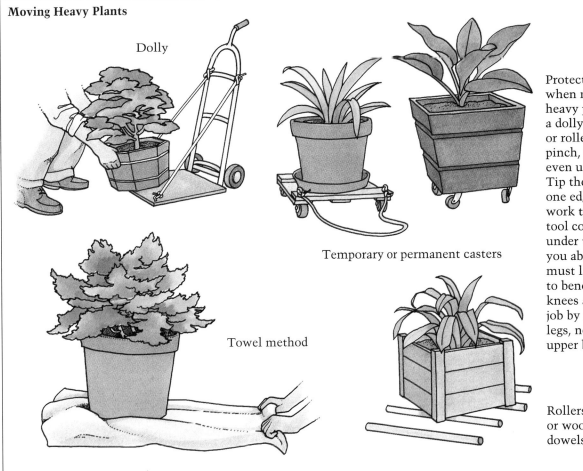

Dolly

Temporary or permanent casters

Towel method

Protect your back when moving heavy plants. Use a dolly, casters, or rollers. In a pinch, you can even use a towel. Tip the pot on one edge, and work the moving tool completely under the pot. If you absolutely must lift, be sure to bend your knees and do the job by using your legs, not your upper body

Rollers of pipe or wooden dowels

It's easy to make your own plant trolley by cutting plywood to size and screwing heavy furniture casters or piano casters to the bottom.

Though a pot may not be large, it may still be too heavy to lift easily. The solution is a tarp or towel. To move the pot without straining your back, spread the towel on the patio, slide the pot onto it, and steady the pot with one hand while pulling slowly with the other. Use an old towel from the ragbag.

If the tub or planter requires two people to lift it, a piece of plywood can make the job easier. Slide the plywood under the planter by tipping the planter first one way and then the other until it is centered on the wood. With one person holding each end (lifting with the legs, not the back), pick up the plywood and carry the planter to its new location.

Buying Plants

In choosing plants, don't look for the biggest or the most floriferous: Look for the healthiest. Big plants in small pots may be root bound. Often, such plants don't transplant well. A plant already covered with flowers will give you a shorter blooming season than one that is well budded, and the process of transplanting a floriferous plant may cause the blooms to droop or drop. The only time it's a good idea to pick plants in full bloom is when they will be slipped, pot and all, into a cachepot for instant color—not transplanted.

Healthy plants have lots of leaves with good color, and their size is in proportion to the pots they are planted in. They may have buds or sturdy new growth. They do not have pests or diseases. Skip the ones with new growth that has died back, yellowing or browning leaves, or foliage that is badly wilted.

Plan your shopping expedition for when you'll have time to pot your purchases within a day or two. Most nursery plants have been grown to transplanting size before being shipped to the nursery—few are improved by being left to sit in their pots for months. Those in six-packs or 4-inch pots are especially vulnerable to drying out or dying back.

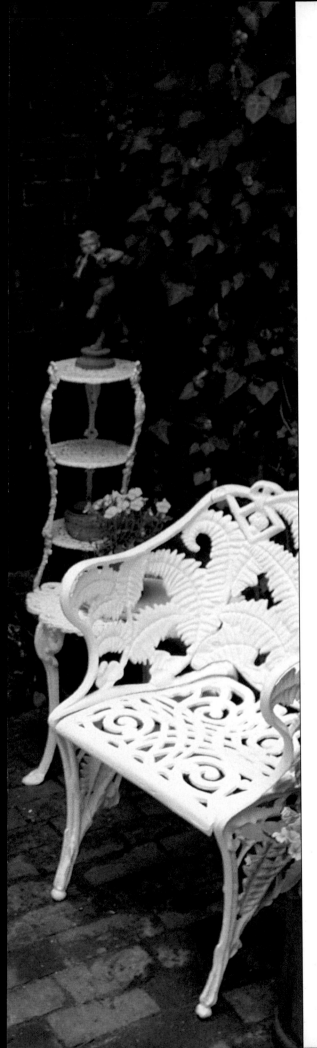

Selecting Your Scene

High-tech furniture or handcrafted bent-willow chairs? Flowered cushions or a stone bench? Have fun browsing through these sample designs and be inspired to transform your balcony, brick square, or wood platform into a gracious and comfortable outdoor room.

This chapter presents a collection of designs for landscaping decks, balconies, and patios—individual scenes complete with recommendations about plants and containers, furniture, and decorations. Adopt a design as it stands, or adapt it to your particular outdoor room. Select the elements that are appropriate to your climate, taste, and life-style. Whatever you choose, the result will be an outdoor living space that can only increase your pleasure in your home.

A romantic retreat has been fashioned from a potted rhododendron and two pieces of furniture in this urban corner.

COLOR FOR ALL SEASONS

A brick or concrete patio that celebrates each season in its turn with a full flush of color calls for plenty of containers. For the most cohesive effect, choose pots with the same style or material: basket-weave concrete pots, familiar English clay flowerpots, or sleek white fiberglass planters, for example. When gardening in a small space, the wise gardener selects plants that have more than one attractive feature or that perform more than once a year. That's the most effective and efficient way to have four seasons of color in the outdoor room.

Spring and Summer

For spring and summer, the greatest impact comes from massing color. Consider, for instance, a planter crammed with velvety red petunias, tall yellow African marigolds, or dark blue salvia. Don't be afraid to crowd nursery seedlings into a pot: Two or three six-packs of annual seedlings to a 6-inch pot work well. Crowded pots require careful monitoring to make sure the soil doesn't dry, however. During hot spells these pots may need daily watering, but they'll give exuberant bloom all summer.

For small, sunny spaces, try a cottage garden in a half-barrel. The tallest plants go in the center, medium-sized plants go in a circle around the tall ones, and small plants that are inclined to sprawl go at the edges to trail over the rim. Put 6-foot double hollyhocks (*Althaea rosea* 'Powderpuff') in the middle; Russell lupines (*Lupinus polyphyllus* Russell hybrids) in a circle around the hollyhocks; and Kenilworth ivy (*Cymbalaria muralis*) on the outside, so it can trail over the edge. A water-thrifty version of this barrel garden includes sky-blue wild indigo (*Baptisia australis*) in the middle, white keys-of-heaven (*Centranthus ruber* 'Albus'), and royal-blue spiderwort (*Tradescantia virginiana* 'Zwanenburg Blue'), all of which are drought tolerant.

To bring butterflies to your balcony, plant a half-barrel with lavender butterfly bush (*Buddleia davidii*) and dusky rose joe-pye-weed (*Eupatorium purpureum*), both of which grow to 5 feet tall. Edge the barrel with pink stonecrop (*Sedum spectabile* 'Meteor'). To attract hummingbirds, plant a red and white honeysuckle (*Lonicera periclymenum* 'Serotina Florida') at one side, where it can climb a post or a trellis against a wall. Fill in the remainder of the barrel with scarlet larkspur (*Delphinium cardinale*), red beebalm (*Monarda didyma*), and red or yellow trailing nasturtium (*Tropaeolum majus*) to tumble over the sides. See the sections called An Urban

These riotous potted plants create a flower border on a deck.

Top left: Bachelor's-buttons (Centaurea cyanus)
Top right: Geraniums (Pelargonium *spp.*), Calceolaria, *and lobelia* (Lobelia erinus) *spilling out of a window box bring an English garden to mind.*
Bottom left: A ruby-throated hummingbird stops at a beebalm (Monarda didyma) *plant.*
Bottom right: Cosmos have a long blooming season and are attractive to butterflies.

Oasis and The Butterfly Farm, later in this chapter, for more about attracting hummingbirds and butterflies.

A simple collection of daylilies (*Hemerocallis*) can create a nearly care-free half-barrel garden, perfect for either a weekend cottage or a very busy gardener. Combine the bright yellow long-blooming miniature 'Stella de Oro' with the sweet-scented soft yellow 'Hyperion' and the yellow-to-white 'My Hope' for bloom from summer through fall. Daylilies are pest-free, tough, hardy, drought tolerant, and undemanding about soil. Simply deadhead spent blossoms regularly and remove the old foliage in the fall, and they'll bloom beautifully for years.

Most of the suggestions so far have been for perennial plants that will die back, be dormant in the winter, and bloom the following year. Annuals provide even more color—more flowers for a longer period—than most perennials, but they need to be replanted annually. In some ways, they're more fun, because you can experiment with new combinations each year. Try a collection of red and purple petunias—plain, ruffled, solid, striped, upright, and trailing. Combine yellow African marigolds (*Tagetes erecta*) with blue bachelor's-buttons (*Centaurea cyanus*), blue Canterbury bells (*Campanula medium*), and yellow creeping zinnias (*Sanvitalia procumbens*). Create a blue garden

Top: Few trees can compete with the fall glory of a Japanese maple (Acer palmatum). Bottom: Shasta daisies (Chrysanthemum maximum) can lengthen the bloom time in your garden.

with blue rocket larkspur (*Consolida ambigua*), Chinese forget-me-not (*Cynoglossum amabile*), summer forget-me-not (*Anchusa capensis*), baby-blue-eyes (*Nemesia menziesii*), and trailing lobelia (*Lobelia erinus* 'Blue Cascade' or 'Sapphire'). A half-barrel of pastel cosmos (*Cosmos bipinnatus* 'Sensation') in pale pink and white looks like an airy impressionist bouquet 6 feet tall.

Fall

The phrase *fall color* typically refers to foliage color rather than flower color, although there are some flowers, shrubs, and vines that bloom in the fall. Most notable among the fall-blooming flowers are the chrysanthemums. They are nearly infinite in their variety, coming in every shape and size from marguerites (*Chrysanthemum frutescens*) to Shasta daisies (*C. × super-*

bum) to florists' mums (*C. morifolium*). Chrysanthemum colors range from white to yellow on through pink, orange, red, lavender, purple, bronze, and multicolored. Other fall-blooming flowers include Japanese anemone (*Anemone × hybrida*), Michaelmas daisy (*Aster*), boltonia (*Boltonia asteroides* 'Snow-bank'), sneezeweed (*Helenium autumnale*), gayfeather (*Liatris*), blue salvia (*Salvia azurea* var. *grandiflora*), pine-apple sage (*S. elegans*), mealycup sage (*S. farinacea* 'Blue Bedder'), scarlet sage (*S. splendens* and *S. × superba* 'East Freisland'), October daphne (*Sedum sieboldii* 'Ruby Glow'), and stonecrop (*S. spectabile* 'Autumn Joy'). On a smaller scale, there are fall-blooming bulbs such as tuberous begonia, canna, autumn crocus (*Colchicum autumnale*), hardy cyclamen, amaryllis (*Lycoris squamigera*), rain-lily (*Zephyranthes grandiflora*), and spider-lily (*Lycoris radiata*). Fall-blooming shrubs include *Camellia sasanqua,* French hydrangea (*Hydrangea macrophylla*), and oleander (*Nerium oleander*). The hardiest fall-blooming vines are sweet autumn clematis (*Clematis maximowicziana*) and virgin's-bower (*C. flammula*).

For shrubs with vibrant fall foliage color, consider witch hazel (*Hamamelis × intermedia* 'Diane'), heavenly bamboo (*Nandina domestica* 'Umpqua Chief'), redosier dogwood (*Cornus sericea × baileyi*), or European cranberry bush (*Viburnum opulus* 'Compactum').

The trees best known for their fall color are Japanese maple (*Acer palmatum*), fernleaf fullmoon maple (*A. japonicum* 'Aconitifolium'), Chinese dogwood (*Cornus kousa* var. *chinensis* 'Milky Way'), Persian parrotia (*Parrotia persica*), Juneberry (*Amelanchier arborea*), sourwood (*Oxydendrum arboreum*), and dwarf white birch (*Betula pendula* 'Trost's Dwarf').

For a patio with great fall color, plant large tubs with trellised sweet autumn clematis underplanted with hardy cyclamen and banked with pots of pink or purple Michaelmas daisies. Bank a large pot containing a scarlet viburnum with pots of big white chrysanthemums. Make an elegant grouping of oriental ceramic pots, one planted with fernleaf fullmoon maple, several planted with heavenly bamboo, and a cobalt-blue bonsai pot with a yellow chrysanthemum cascade. Espalier a *Camellia sasanqua* on a patio wall and underplant it with small ferns. Let white virgin's-bower clamber over an arch or arbor, and place big pots of lace-cap French hydrangea at the base of the posts. (Hydrangea flowers are blue in acidic soil [pH 5.0 to 5.5] with available aluminum; they are pink in alkaline soil [pH 6.0 and above].) A mild-climate window box could cascade luxuriantly with velvet-red tuberous begonias. Rectangular planters thick with scarlet sage or dark blue sage can be set off to perfection with 12-inch pots of pineapple sage at either end. Celebrate native American flowers with white *Boltonia asteroides* 'Snowbank', deep-purple New England aster (*Aster novae-angliae*), blue mealycup sage, and blue-violet New York aster (*A. novi-belgii*) in big blue and white graniteware tin washtubs. Clumped under a tubbed sourwood tree in brilliant scarlet fall foliage, this all-American show is—appropriately enough—red, white, and blue.

Winter

Don't forget the patio in winter. Evergreens are one way to keep some color and life in the winter garden. Evergreens needn't be green—some are blue, others yellow, and still others variegated. Tom Thumb arborvitae (*Thuja occidentalis* 'Globosa', 'Little Gem', 'Little Giant', and 'Nana', which are all green) rarely grow to more than 3 feet in height, but they need protection from winter wind and cold in severe climates. Dwarf oriental arborvitae (*Platycladus orientalis* 'Aureus') are compact, globular, and golden. *P. orientalis* 'Bakeri' is bright green and shaped like a cone, and 'Bonita' grows to form a rounded cone about 3 feet tall that's dark green with a touch of gold at the tips. False arborvitae (*Thujopsis dolabrata* 'Nana') grows very slowly, an advantage in a container plant; 'Nana' is green, but the cultivar 'Variegata' has green branchlets tipped with white.

Two varieties of deodar cedar (*Cedrus deodara*), 'Descanso Dwarf' and 'Prostrata', are useful for deck or patio container planting. Both are a gray-green that approaches blue. Port Orford cedar, also called Lawson cypress (*Chamaecyparis lawsonia*), has several blue dwarf forms: silver-gray 'Azurea', silver-gray 'Ellwoodii Improved', and blue-green 'Minima Glauca'. None of these grows much higher than 8 feet, and all grow slowly. One form of nootka cypress, also called Alaska yellow cypress (*C. nootkatensis*), is well suited for life in a container. It is the blue-green 'Compacta', which grows to only 3 feet. The yellow-green 'Pendula', which grows to 10 feet in 10 years, can eventually reach 30 feet. When it outgrows the patio or terrace, plant it out in the garden or give it to a friend with a large yard. Fernspray cypress (*C. obtusa* 'Filicoides'), which is medium green, eventually grows to 15 feet and is invaluable for oriental-style gardens. Slender Hinoki cypress (*C. obtusa* 'Gracilis'), a glossy dark green, is very slow-growing and is excellent in large containers. Eventually, it can reach a height of 20 feet. *C. obtusa* 'Kosteri', 'Nana', 'Nana Aurea', and 'Nana Gracilis' are superb in containers; none exceeds 4 feet in height. All are dark green except 'Nana Aurea', on which new growth is yellow and old growth is dark green. English yew (*Taxus baccata*), another excellent evergreen, comes in several dwarf forms. 'Standishii' is often considered the best golden yew; 'Nana' and 'Pygmea' are green. *T. baccata* 'Nana' grows to only 3 feet. A taller choice is *T. cuspidata* 'Nana', which grows very slowly to 6 feet. Japanese black pine (*Pinus thunbergiana*) is exceptionally suited to a container; it is one of the classic bonsai trees. Left to its own devices, it will eventually grow to 30 feet or more, but pruning can keep it substantially smaller for many years.

Small trees and shrubs with berries are another way to strike a bright note in winter. As a bonus, many of them attract birds, which add

The winter garden has its own charm. Deciduous trees and shrubs drop their leaves, exposing their branch structure. The roses are gone, but the rock wall they concealed is more evident. The garden is more open, bringing in the surrounding countryside. It seems less private, but more a part of its surroundings. Notice how the clipped evergreeen shrubs, almost hidden in the summer garden, dominate the winter garden scene.

life, movement, and charm to dark winter days. A disease-resistant crabapple with glossy cherry-red fruit until frost is the National Arboretum cultivar *Malus* 'Narragansett'. The weeping *Malus* 'Red Jade' has bright red fruits that last into winter, but it is less disease resistant than 'Narragansett'. Firethorn (*Pyracantha coccinea*) covers itself with masses of red or yellow fruit; in the late winter and early spring, flocks of robins make themselves tipsy on the berries. Recommended cultivars include the bright red 'Mohave' and clear yellow 'Shawnee', which espalier well, and 'Red Elf' ('Leprechaun') and 'Tiny Tim', which are small enough for container growing.

Holly berries also attract robins and other songbirds. A number of hollies have variegated foliage that provides winter color in addition to that of the berries. Chinese holly (*Ilex cornuta*

'Berries Jubilee') is a dwarf form with a natural dome shape; 'Dazzler' is compact and upright. Neither needs a pollinator for it to bear lots of bright red berries. Japanese holly (*I. crenata*) has black berries, which are striking against the gold leaves of *I. crenata* 'Golden Heller'. Dwarf yaupon holly (*Ilex vomitoria* 'Nana') is a refined-looking and exceptionally attractive plant. It grows to 1½ feet and can bear heavily without a pollinator. A blue holly with purple stems is *I. × meserveae,* which grows to 7 feet. Female plants need a pollinator to produce berries. Of the female plants, 'Blue Angel', 'Blue Girl', and 'Blue Princess' are fine choices; male pollinators are 'Blue Boy', 'Blue Stallion', and 'Blue Prince'. English holly, the traditional Christmas holly (*I. aquifolium*), is dioecious: Males must be present for female plants to bear fruit. English holly grows slowly, but it will

eventually outgrow its container. Choice cultivars for berries are 'Angustifolia' and 'Sparkler'. Effective male pollinators are 'Little Bull' and 'Gold Coast'; the latter has bright yellow edging on dark green leaves. Variegated hollies come in either silver or gold. 'Argenteo-marginata' and 'Silver King' are edged with silver; 'Aurea–Medio-picta' and 'Silver Star' have silver-centered leaves. 'Aureo-marginata' and 'Lily Gold' have gold-edged leaves; 'Golden Milkmaid' and 'Pinto' have leaves with gold centers. 'Sparkleberry' is a deciduous hybrid introduced by the National Arboretum. Its brilliantly shiny, long-lasting berries are especially dramatic after the leaves fall, particularly when seen against fresh snow. Plant with a male, such as 'Apollo', to get the most berries.

Cotoneasters can be neglected. They actually flower and fruit better in poor, dry soil than in rich, moist soil. Some are small trees or shrubs, others are ground covers. Try red clusterberry (*Cotoneaster lacteus*) in a large box or as an espalier. The best pick for a container plant is the ground cover *C. congestus* 'Likiang' or the bearberry cotoneaster, *C. dammeri.*

Toyon (*Heteromeles arbutifolia*) has long-lasting red berries all through the winter, as does the strawberry tree (*Arbutus unedo*). *A. unedo* 'Elfin King' is a picturesque, contorted true dwarf, barely 5 feet tall. It is an especially choice container plant. Not only does 'Elfin King' flower and fruit almost continuously, but the rich shaggy reddish bark on gnarled, twisted branches offers an interesting silhouette and texture.

Achieve a striking contemporary look with variegated hollies in black glazed cylindrical pots. Combine black-fruited Japanese holly 'Golden Heller' with pots of red-fruited dwarf yaupon holly. Add a large scarlet 'Sparkleberry' where it can be lighted at night. Or go after the same effect with a combination of the gold- and silver-leafed hollies. Tie the pots with French wire ribbons in big bows, and you'll have a sophisticated Christmas presentation.

Sacred bamboo (*Nandina domestica*) produces sprays of red berries that hold all winter. *Sarcococca ruscifolia* has very fragrant white flowers that turn into red fruit. It is extremely slow-growing—only 6 inches a year—and invaluable in heavily shaded areas. It makes a neat, orderly hedge or forms a natural espalier planted against a wall. These plants contribute

more than just winter interest. Sacred bamboo, for example, has delicate sprays of tiny white flowers in the spring and excellent color in the fall. The flowers of *Sarcococca* are inconspicuous, but wonderfully fragrant.

Two rare and choice native American trees, more widely grown in England than in the United States, are *Franklinia alatahama* and *Stewartia pseudocamellia.* Franklinia has fragrant white flowers from August until frost. The tree may still be blooming when the leaves turn crimson, giving an unusual and spectacular summer and fall show. Stewartia has white camellia-like flowers in July; fall colors of red, yellow, and purple; and a beautiful bark pattern of gray to orange-brown all year.

The red berries of this cotoneaster make an agreeable contrast with the snow. The plant shown here, Cotoneaster horizontalis, *can grow to 10 feet wide. Bearberry cotoneaster (C. dammeri), clusterberry (C. lacteus), and the ground cover* C. congestus *are varieties more suited to containers.*

EDIBLE LANDSCAPES

The fact is that many fruits and vegetables are extremely attractive. Tomatoes were thought to be poisonous and were grown in Europe only as ornamentals for centuries before anyone dared eat them. Queen-Anne's-lace, one of the loveliest wildflowers, is nothing more than a carrot gone wild.

A tremendous amount of hybridizing has been done to miniaturize both fruit and vegetable plants. Fruit trees come in three sizes of small: semi-dwarf, dwarf, and genetic dwarf. Semi-dwarf trees grow 12 to 15 feet tall, dwarf trees grow 8 to 10 feet tall, and genetic dwarfs rarely get taller than 8 feet, though all bear full-sized fruit. Bean, squash, melon, and cucumber plants that used to sprawl all over now come in compact bush forms. Carrot plants that once required 10 inches of loose, friable topsoil now produce a round crop that can easily be grown in a window box. Tomatoes also come in container sizes: One hybrid is even named 'Patio'.

Grapes are traditionally grown on an arbor over a patio. Grapevines endure for many years;

Artichokes are pleasing to the eye as well as the palate. The raised bed in the background contains beans and strawberries.

have tremendous character; color attractively in the fall; and of course, produce grapes. Is there a more sensuous picture of abundance than vines heavy with ripe grapes that hang down from an overhead arbor?

Artichoke and asparagus plants are striking, irrespective of the fact that the vegetables they produce taste good and qualify as gourmet foods. Both need big, sturdy tubs or planters, and both last for years. Artichokes have close-lapped gray-green buds (the part that is eaten) and, if they are permitted to bloom, immense purple thistle-like flowers. Fresh, the flowers are superb in arrangements, and they can be used dried in bouquets as well. They need cold-weather protection in harsh climates.

The part of the asparagus plant that ends up on your plate is the immature leafstalk. Left to grow, the familiar spears open out into delicate, feathery leaves that bear tiny sprays of white flowers. The effect is of a thick bank of tall, graceful ferns. Establishing crop-bearing plants takes patience, but the reward of fresh asparagus can make the effort worthwhile. Using a half-barrel or deep planter, lay three-year-old asparagus roots, sold by nurseries, in a 6-inch-deep trench of loose manure-enriched soil. Cover them with 2 inches of soil initially. As the spears grow, fill in around them until they're covered to a depth of 6 inches, taking care not to bury the growing tips. Let them grow the first year into their delicate, airy foliage. Harvest lightly the second year and for 8 to 10 weeks the third year. (Spears should be 5 to 8 inches long before they're cut.) After each spring's harvest, let the asparagus leaf out for the summer and fall. Male varieties such as 'Jersey Giant' and 'UC 157' tend to produce substantially heavier crops than female varieties such as 'Mary Washington'.

Herbs are essential to the edible landscape, and a number of them are extremely ornamental. Parsley (*Petroselinum crispum*) has crisp, green leaves that make a superior edging in a flower bed bordering a patio. Creeping thyme (*Thymus serphyllum*) can grow between paving stones on a path leading from house to patio or from patio to garden. Dwarf dill (*Anethum graveolens* 'Fernleaf') gives the effect of ferns but thrives in sun where most ferns falter. Lavender (*Lavandula angustifolia* 'Munstead') makes a handsome low hedge to set off a flagstone patio from the lawn.

Left: Monarch butterflies are especially attracted to Asclepias tuberosa, *which is called, appropriately enough, butterfly weed. Right: Quite a lot of fruit can be grown in a strawberry planter. You may find that butterflies aren't the only ones attracted.*

The Butterfly Farm

One of the nice things about a butterfly garden is that many of the edibles that attract butterflies are delicious to humans. Cherries, blueberries, passionflower, sage, fennel, chives, parsley, and sunflowers all attract butterflies in addition to being useful in the kitchen. On a sunny patio, add the self-pollinating dwarf cherry tree (Starkrimson® Sweet) in a big tub where it can eventually reach its full height of 14 feet. Under the cherry tree, plant sweet violets (*Viola odorata* 'Royal Robe'). Hedge opposite sides of the patio with two different kinds of blueberry ('Bluecrop' and 'Earliblue'). Mulch thickly to keep the shallow roots cool and patio edges neat and tidy. Where the patio joins the back lawn, hedge with lavender to a central arch, and grow climbing roses over the arch. If a nearby window receives a lot of sun, plant a window box of scarlet sage (*Salvia splendens*). The flowers lure butterflies, as do pots of red valerian (*Centranthus ruber*). The pale yellow flowers of Algerian ivy (*Hedera canariensis*) attract honeybees as well as butterflies—skippers, painted ladies, and monarchs among them. Next to the house, place a long rectangular planter with a trellis in the center. Plant a passionflower (*Passiflora edulis* 'Incense') to climb and cover the trellis; this passionflower variety has flowers 5 inches across, a fragrance reminiscent of sweet peas, and edible fruit. Plant the remainder of the planter with alpine strawberries, the ones the French call *fraises des bois* ('Baron Solemacher'): It takes lots of plants to get enough of these tiny wild strawberries for breakfast. Bank the cherry tree with pots of dill, fennel, pineapple sage, parsley, and chives.

Water is as essential to butterflies as it is to birds and other creatures. Make sure to provide a water source in your butterfly garden. It might be a formal birdbath, a wall fountain, or a simple 14-inch terra-cotta saucer that you fill daily with fresh water. The butterflies will balance on the rim of the water container, sip delicately, and open their wings to show off their beautiful colors and patterns.

If that display weren't enough, your butterfly garden will provide you with cherry blossoms and violets in the spring and roses, passionflowers, and spikes of purple lavender in the summer. There will be cherries in May, alpine strawberries in June and July, and blueberries in August, as well as a variety of herbs for most of the summer. The roses, passionflowers, lavender, and herbs will all contribute their sweet fragrance to the outdoor room. A table with chairs and perhaps a chaise lounge are all that are needed to make this outdoor room comfortable as well as pleasant.

Remember, however, that butterflies mean caterpillars. Those fluttering jewels are not merely innocently sipping nectar; they are also laying eggs. Be prepared to spend some time handpicking them to send to school with the children as a science project.

The Rooftop Farm

The serious farmer who happens to live in a city may have to cultivate a rooftop garden. Check with the building owner or manager before you begin. Some ordinances and building

Left: A potted vegetable garden can be moved to take advantage of light or other conditions that change with the season.
Right: Raised beds raise the level of the garden, making the task of gardening easier and more pleasant.

codes prohibit rooftop gardening, so before plunging ahead ask the local building department also. It is essential that the roof be able to support the extra weight of the garden, which will be substantial. Equally essential is easy access to water. You'll need to hook up a hose somewhere, either to a spigot or an indoor tap. Carrying water up in buckets or watering cans is out of the question. Water is heavy and hard to carry without spilling, and the task is exhausting. In addition, find out if you will need electricity or gas in the rooftop garden and determine the best way to supply it.

Be sure the roof is watertight *before* you start your garden. Some roofing surfaces, specifically tar paper or tar and gravel, don't stand up well to foot traffic or contact with sharp objects such as the corner of a container or the legs of a table. To protect the roof, buy wooden decking. It is relatively simple to install on a flat roof. Many building emporiums carry duckboard, prefabricated squares of wooden decking that can be laid down to suit the space. Wooden decking not only improves the appearance of a rooftop garden, but it absorbs less heat than tar paper or tar-and-gravel roofing, making the garden significantly cooler and more comfortable for people and plants.

One of the best things about rooftop gardening is that there's plenty of sun. Urban yards, patios, and balconies may be shaded by high-rise neighbors, but rooftop gardens don't often have that particular problem. In fact, the rooftop garden may need an arbor or shady retreat of some kind, where you can sit and contemplate your work.

Wind can present serious difficulties, since rooftops are so exposed. Plants in a windy location need frequent watering, since wind strips moisture from leaves. Some plants may require staking to keep them from blowing over. Building a windbreak is another way to solve the problem of wind. A tailored evergreen hedge, a windbreak of small trees, or a lath fence that can double as a trellis can make it easier to grow plants. It can also make the rooftop garden more comfortable for the gardener and, as a fringe benefit, provide additional privacy for relaxing, entertaining, or sunbathing. Privacy is an especially welcome bonus in a crowded city.

One other important consideration is air pollution. Leaves become coated with dust and soot. Rooftop plants need to be rinsed off frequently with a fine spray so they can "breathe" (transpire) and photosynthesize. Some plants don't tolerate smog well, particularly Japanese

maples, some species of orchids, and rhododendrons. Food plants that don't tolerate excessively smoggy conditions include apple and citrus trees, grapevines, and bean and tomato plants. If conditions are smoggy where you live, petunias serve well as indicators. If the petunia leaves are flecked with silver and there are no insects around that are clearly responsible, it's reasonable to suspect that heavy smog has caused the damage. In such a case, rinse your plants often and wash any fruits or vegetables carefully before eating them.

In spite of all the extra care you need to take, rooftop urban farming can be enormously rewarding. As one indomitable gardener observed, in any given city, rooftops represent acres of unused space. And there are certain undeniable advantages to rooftop gardening. For example, snails and slugs are unlikely to cause many problems, and gophers, rabbits, and deer never present any difficulty.

Suppose your rooftop area is 16 by 24 feet. To get your rooftop garden off to a good start, plant semi-dwarf or dwarf fruit trees in large wooden tubs or terra-cotta pots, three along each side. Consider peaches or nectarines on dwarfing rootstock or one of the genetic dwarf peaches, which have a natural Japanese bonsai appearance. A wide variety of apples is available on dwarfing rootstock, as are dwarf sweet cherries. Underplant three of the trees with June-bearing strawberries, which trail their runners over the edge of the tub with casual abandon, and the other three with runnerless alpine strawberries, the European wild strawberry with intense strawberry flavor.

Next, build six planters in position between the tubs. Each should be 18 inches wide, 6 feet long, and 30 inches deep. Fill the planters with a light potting mix. Plant four of them with bush varieties of watermelon, rhubarb, and summer and winter squash. 'Bush Acorn Table King', 'Butterbush', and the spaghetti squash 'Tivoli Hybrid' are comparatively compact, long-keeping winter squashes. Bush zucchini and 'White Patty Pan' are prolific summer squashes. 'Bush Sugar Baby' is a dwarf watermelon vine that produces fruit 10½ inches around; each 'Honeybush' cantaloupe is only 7 inches across but bears full-sized fruit; and 'MacDonald' rhubarb has brilliant red, exceptionally sweet stalks. In between the squash and watermelon, plant yellow calendulas or pungent French

marigolds as companion plants to keep the pest population down. They are edible in their own right and provide a bright spot of color in the garden. You can plant vining nasturtiums—with edible leaves and equally edible red, orange, or yellow flowers—so they drape over the edges of the planters.

Along one 16-foot side of the rooftop garden, nail 6-foot-high lattice to the back of two 6-foot-long planters. This is where all the clambering, climbing, vining plants go: tomato, pea, bean, cucumber, sweet potato, Malabar spinach (*Basella alba*), and melon. Simply secure them to the lattice with plant ties as they grow. Underplant with lettuce and spinach in spring, Swiss chard and New Zealand spinach (*Tetragonia expansa*) in summer. Using vertical space this way accomplishes two purposes: More can be grown in a small space, and the vine-covered lattice effectively blocks views that are less than scenic.

Top: Rhubarb would be worth growing for its becoming leaves even if the stems were inedible.
Bottom: Espaliers protect fruit from wind and take up little space. You need not use a wall; you can use a trellis.

This urban balcony could easily contain potted vegetables or herbs.

A pot of tomatoes can contribute a surprising amount of salad material.

Wise choices for the lattice are the exotic yellow and silver oriental melons 'Early Silver Line', which *Burpee's Seed Catalog* describes as "crisp, sweet and fragrant"; Armenian cucumbers, with their strangely ribbed texture; petits pois (small peas) 'Petit Provenal', which will fruit in either spring or fall; and sugar peas 'Mammoth Melting Sugar', which are incredibly expensive at the supermarket and ridiculously easy to grow at home. Also include snap peas 'Sugar Snap', which can be eaten either with the pods when young or without when mature, and sweet potatoes 'Centennial', which can be dug as early as 90 days or left until just before frost.

Tomatoes are a whole category unto themselves. By far the most popular homegrown vegetable, they come in a welter of sizes, shapes, and colors for every conceivable purpose: salad tomatoes, cherry tomatoes, beefsteak tomatoes, paste tomatoes, patio tomatoes, early tomatoes, late tomatoes, long-keeping tomatoes, red tomatoes, pink tomatoes, orange tomatoes, and yellow tomatoes. Choose according to what you want to use them for: beefsteaks for hamburgers and hero sandwiches; regular-sized tomatoes to slice for salads; cherry tomatoes for cool summer antipasto plates; long-keeping tomatoes if you want fresh tomatoes through fall and into winter; and paste tomatoes for marinara sauce, catsup, or canning. The best paste tomatoes are 'Roma VF' and 'San Marzano'. Recommended yellow tomatoes are 'Yellow Pear' and 'Lemon Boy'. The sweetest vining cherry tomato is 'Super Sweet 100'. A classic salad tomato plant is 'Burpee's Big Girl® VF', which can grow fruits that weigh a pound apiece. If you are an urban farmer who dreams of someday winning the blue ribbon at the county fair, grow 'Delicious', which produced the world's biggest tomato. That tomato weighed a record 7 pounds, 12 ounces, according to the *Guinness Book of World Records*.

Remember, a few tomato plants can produce a stupendous (or stupefying) number of tomatoes. Either restrict yourself to two or three plants or plan to donate some of your crop to the local food bank. Tomatoes have a tendency to ripen all at once, and they need to be eaten or canned within a few days of ripening.

Obviously, there are more vegetables to grow than room to grow them in a 16- by 24-foot garden. Only grow those vegetables you know your family will eat; it's foolish to waste space on food nobody likes. For a family of four, two tomato vines, two pea vines, two cucumber vines, two melon vines, and two sweet-potato vines would produce a rich bounty of fresh vegetables from spring into fall. Since peas are a cool-weather crop, spring-planted peas will be spent by mid-June. Pull the peas out and plant the sweet potatoes in their place; sweet potatoes love warm weather, and they'll grow until frost.

Make wooden lids for the planters to transform them into benches when the summer crops are done. Warm-climate urban farmers can plant cool-weather crops to grow from fall through winter. Vegetable plants that grow well in frost-free areas include lettuce, spinach, chard, broccoli, broccoli romanesco, cauliflower, raddichio, head cabbage, bok choy, oriental cabbage, Florence fennel (also called finocchio), pea, carrot, parsnip, turnip, and rutabaga.

The rooftop garden described in this chapter is highly ornamental as well as highly productive. In the spring, the fruit trees burst into bloom, scattering pale petals on the deck and benches. The leaves of the squash and rhubarb are huge and richly verdant. The strawberry plants have small white flowers; the yellow squash blossoms are delicately etched with green; peas have fragile white sweet-pea–like blooms; sweet-potato vines have morning-glory flowers and heart-shaped leaves; and the nasturtium, marigold, and calendula are hummingbird red, chrome yellow, or pumpkin orange.

A table, a chair or two, and an umbrella to shelter from the sun is all the furniture this outdoor rooftop room needs. It's the perfect place to putter for an hour in the morning, sipping a cup of hot coffee, before plunging into the commuter war. It's a delicious place to relax on a long summer evening, savoring a sun-warm peach. A rooftop garden is a private piece of country hidden high above the city.

The Patio Plantation

An edible landscape can be incorporated into any patio or terrace by planting combinations of edibles and ornamentals in half-barrels, pots, strawberry pots, or window boxes. Make an herb garden in a strawberry pot: Plant rosemary in the center and tuck thyme, tarragon, sage, summer savory, sweet marjoram, and oregano into the pockets. Delight a child with pots of dwarf sunflowers (*Helianthus annuus* 'Sunspot'): They're only 18 inches tall, but the flowers are a foot across. When the flowers have set seed, put a couple of the pots where the birds can feast on them—then eat the rest of the seeds yourself. Plant a big pot of garlic. (Roasted garlic is sweet, not sharp, and absolutely wonderful squeezed and mashed onto toast rounds brushed with olive oil.)

Landscape a playhouse with trees to scale by planting miniature fruit trees. Or screen the children's sandbox or play yard with a hedge of genetic dwarf fruit trees. Maybe the children will pick themselves a ripe peach instead of coming inside to wheedle cookies.

If you have a balcony with an ugly view, plant a long planter with Jerusalem artichokes (sunchokes). They'll block the view by growing 8 feet tall, and they have blooms like small sunflowers. Sunchoke blooms make big, handsome country-style bouquets. In the late fall, harvest the tubers to chop them raw for salads, float a single translucent slice on consommé laced with sherry, dice them for turkey dressing, or cook them any way you would potatoes.

Strawberry pots make interesting planters for herbs or lettuces.

Amazingly, the fruit of dwarf trees is often almost full-size. In ornamental pots, the trees make a dramatic impression.

Plant a window box with white jonquil bulbs and curly parsley seedlings in the fall. The jonquils will bloom early in the spring and the parsley will stay fresh and green all winter. As soon as the jonquils are past bloom, poke in a few seeds of variegated nasturtium 'Alaska'. The parsley is for garnish and seasoning; the nasturtium flowers and leaves are for summer salads.

The Miniature Orchard

Semi-dwarf fruit trees are tall enough to provide some summer shade in addition to fruit. With the flowers they provide in spring, fruit trees give the gardener three seasons of beauty and usefulness. Dwarf trees don't provide much shade, but their fruit is easy to harvest. Miniature fruit trees are the best choice where space is at a premium. Even the smallest balcony could accommodate a little urban orchard of three or four 24-inch pots. Peach, nectarine, apricot, pear, and apple trees are all available in miniature sizes. All these—plus plum, cherry, Asian pear, pluot (a cross between plum and apricot), aprium (this one is more apricot than plum), and almond—are available in dwarf sizes. It's possible to grow six dwarf fruit trees in a space 16 by 24 feet. If a half-dozen spaces for trees were left in a brick patio, you could dine under the canopy of your patio orchard and pick dessert from the table!

Though persimmons eventually outgrow containers, they are an exceptionally attractive small tree. Persimmons give pleasant shade in summer, and they color richly in fall, even in warm climates; the shiny golden fruit hangs on after the leaves have fallen. The branches have an attractive winter silhouette. To prevent ripe fruit from falling or being eaten by birds, pick the fruit a little underripe. It ripens at room temperature and looks spectacular in a basket as a centerpiece. To ripen persimmons fast, put them in the freezer overnight; they'll be soft-ripe by morning. (Underripe persimmons are very astringent.) The most attractive oriental persimmon is *Diospyros kaki* 'Hachiya'.

There are a few things to remember about fruit trees as patio or deck or balcony trees. They may drop overripe fruit, if it's not picked regularly, and make a mess. Plopped plums and peaches attract bees and wasps. Ripe fruit also attracts birds, so plan on using bird netting (an effective but not very attractive solution). Another solution is to use bird scares, shiny tin shapes hung in the branches to frighten birds off. (Scares are a more attractive but less effective measure than netting.) Or, accept that birds and squirrels will get more than their fair share of fruit. Be sure that the fruit trees you choose are self-pollinating or that there are other fruit trees in the neighborhood. To be

certain of pollination, buy two different varieties of the same fruit tree. Fruit trees also need spraying to prevent diseases and to control pests. Look for disease-resistant varieties—such as 'Jonafree', 'Liberty', and 'Prima' apple trees—to keep spraying to a minimum.

The Orangerie

Citrus may come as close as any single tree can to being perfect. They are handsomely shaped, the leaves are glossy and evergreen, the flowers are lovely, the fragrance is legendary, and the fruits are both delicious and long-keeping. Citrus trees need warmth to set fruit and must winter at temperatures above 25° F. In cool climates they can be brought into a greenhouse, atrium, sunroom, or brightly lighted basement or garage for the winter. If trees are wintered indoors, give them very little water.

Sweet orange trees (*Citrus sinensis*), the source of the ubiquitous breakfast orange juice, are native to southern China and Vietnam. Sweet oranges are so common in supermarkets today, it's hard to believe they were rare in 1900. Oranges were a luxury only the rich could afford, a treasured treat in a Christmas stocking, to be saved and savored.

The most commonly grown citrus in China is the mandarin orange (*Citrus reticulata*). Mandarins include tangerines, which have loose, red-orange peels, and satsumas, which have light yellow peels. The third type of orange, the bitter orange *Citrus aurantium,* is the variety used for marmalade or heavily sweetened orangeade.

Hot summers are necessary for citrus to set fruit; mild winters are essential to survival. Of the Citrus family, lemon trees and lime trees need the least amount of heat to produce good fruit. Orange trees need high summer temperatures to set fruit, with navel orange trees requiring more heat than Valencias. (Navel oranges are the thick-peeled eating kind; Valencia oranges are the thin-peeled fruit used for juice.) Grapefruit only develops full-flavored fruit where there are long, hot summers, such as California, Arizona, Texas, and Florida. From hardiest to least hardy, the citrus rank in this order: calamondin, kumquat, orangequat, bitter orange, 'Owari' mandarin, 'Improved Meyer' lemon, 'Rangpur' lime, most tangerines, sweet orange, 'Bearss' lime, tangelo and tangor, regular lemon, pummelo, grapefruit, limequat, and 'Mexican' lime. Calamondin can take temperatures as low as 20° F; 'Mexican' lime will tolerate temperatures no lower than 28° F.

Like roses, citrus prefer moist soil, but sulk when they have wet feet. Plenty of water with fast drainage is the essential combination for citrus to thrive. Since most citrus grown on decks and patios are potted and most potting mixes are fairly fast draining, drainage is not

Left: Even before the fruit ripens, Marsh seedless grapefruit are attractive.
Right: Dwarf lemon trees grace a formal Italian garden. Lemons are the easiest of the citrus to grow in cooler zones. However, they should be moved indoors when temperatures remain below freezing.

The delicate scent of the blossoms is reason enough to grow citrus trees.

The likely culprits are aphids, mealybugs, mites, and the bugs that produce scale. Where summers are very hot, the bark on citrus trunks can sunburn. Either wrap the trunk with commercial tree-wrap paper, which is available at nurseries and garden centers, or paint it with brown or gray cold-water wall paint. Use the color that best approximates the natural color of the trunk.

Few courtyards or patios are big enough for standard-sized trees, which can grow up to 30 feet high and 30 feet wide. Dwarf trees are a better choice, especially for container planting, since they are generally only 4 to 10 feet in height and width. Dwarf citrus trees may be grafted on one of two different rootstocks: trifoliate orange (*Poncirus trifoliata*) or Hiryu (*P. monstrasa* 'Flying Dragon'). Trees grown on trifoliate orange understocks develop into trees 4 to 10 feet tall; those grown on Hiryu tend to be smaller, growing from 5 to 7 feet tall. If the height or spread makes a big difference in your plan, find out which rootstock the tree was grafted on. Keep an eye out for suckers that sprout below the graft and cut them all flush with the trunk; if you don't, they'll overwhelm the tree.

As the word *orangerie* suggests, oranges are the citrus traditionally grown in formal collections in Italy, France, and England. The best oranges for eating are dwarf 'Washington' and 'Robertson' navels. 'Washington' bears fruit from December to February. 'Robertson' orange trees bear two to three weeks earlier and produce amazing amounts of fruit. For juice oranges, choose dwarf 'Valencia' and 'Shamouti' ('Palestine Jaffa'). 'Shamouti' fruit is seedless and the dwarf tree has an exceptionally beautiful form and foliage.

The sour oranges don't come on dwarf rootstock, since few people want an orange tree with oranges so sour. Nevertheless, they can be pruned heavily to create impenetrable, deliciously fragrant hedges. The fruit of the Seville orange is a spectacular orange-red, and it is the source of the very finest bitter marmalade.

Blood oranges have red fruit and juice, and tend to be considered a gourmet item if they are available in grocery stores. They thrive wherever oranges grow well. The 'Moro' tree bears fruit from January to April, and 'Sanguinelli' bears from February to May. So, for five months of fancy blood oranges, grow both.

ordinarily a problem. Sufficient water in hot-summer areas is more likely to be the dilemma, so be sure a hose is within easy reach or put citrus on an automatic drip-mist system. Water twice a week in summer, and as often as daily during a heat wave.

Citrus tend to be shallow rooted, so some sort of mulch is a wise idea. Consider a living mulch of Corsican mint (*Mentha requienii*), Australian violet (*Viola hederacea*), or blue star-creeper (*Laurentia fluviatilis*) in classic terra-cotta pots. A striking mulch is a 2- to 3-inch layer of small shiny black or white river rocks, particularly in contemporary glazed, cylindrical pots.

Citrus use a lot of nitrogen, so fertilize with a high-nitrogen fertilizer two or three times a year, in late winter, June, or August. Most pests can be controlled with a hard spray of water:

'Eureka' is the standard supermarket lemon. 'Lisbon' lemons are practically identical, but the tree that produces them tolerates greater extremes of heat and cold. Both varieties bear fruit the year around, though 'Lisbon' ripens most of its fruit in the fall. 'Sungold' is a semi-dwarf variant that grows to 14 feet tall and 8 feet wide. It is of interest because of its intriguing green-striped yellow fruit and variegated cream-and-green leaves. 'Ponderosa' is a curious novelty, with huge, rough-skinned fruit; each lemon can easily weigh 2 pounds. The dwarf grows 4 to 6 feet tall and bears most of its fruit in the winter. The lemons it produces aren't very juicy, but their rinds are superb for lemon zest.

A 'Bearss' lime is nearly the size of a lemon, pale yellow, seedless, and very juicy. The tree produces some fruit all year, but the majority of the fruit ripens in winter and spring. Dwarf trees grow from 7 to 10 feet tall and have a dense round crown at maturity. Unfortunately for the purposes of formal display, 'Bearss' has the unpleasant habit of dropping most of its leaves in the winter. 'Mexican', the familiar green bartender's lime, is the least hardy of all citrus—it must have warm winters (above freezing) or greenhouse protection to survive.

The loose, puckered skin of tangerines or mandarin oranges is easy to peel, and the fruit inside is deliciously sweet. The standard supermarket tangerine is 'Dancy', which begins ripening in December—in time to be tucked into Christmas stockings along with almonds and walnuts. The tree is especially attractive in containers and, unlike other varieties, doesn't require another variety for pollination. 'Kinnow' bears fruit a bit larger than 'Dancy', with a rich fragrance and flavor. It has fruit from January through May, and the dwarf is a symmetrical, thickly leaved columnar tree that grows to 10 feet. The fruit of 'Owari' is the satsuma orange used to make canned mandarin oranges. It has a sweet, delicate flavor and ripens earlier than any others—from October to Christmas. Dwarf trees make interesting 6-foot shrubs that start out open and angular and get more compact with age. The fruits keep well in cool storage.

Kumquat trees are handsome whether or not they bloom and fruit—they may not flower or fruit where winters are cold. On dwarf rootstock, they make a compact 4-foot shrub or

Kumquat trees, like other citrus, can be pruned to a desired shape and placed in ornamental pots.

tree. The leaves are bright green, the flowers richly fragrant, and the edible rind somewhat sweet; the fruit itself is tart. It's better in marmalade than eaten fresh. 'Meiwa' has round, comparatively sweet fruit.

A calamondin tree is extremely attractive in a container, growing 8 to 10 feet and bearing hundreds of tiny orange fruit—which are, unfortunately, primarily ornamental. The fruit is too sour to eat fresh, but it makes a superior and exotic marmalade. What a marvelous Christmas gift homemade calamondin marmalade would be!

A Rangpur lime is not a lime at all. It doesn't taste like a lime, and it looks and peels like a tangerine. It adds an interesting flavor to regular lemonade and is highly ornamental the year around. Dwarf Rangpur lime trees grow quickly to 8 feet and are vigorous, sturdy, and dense when pruned.

The best dwarf tangelo (a hybrid of the 'Dancy' tangerine and grapefruit) is the big, bright orange 'Mineola'. It ripens in February and March and is virtually seedless. 'Temple' is a dwarf tangor, a cross between a tangerine and an orange. The fruit is tender, juicy, and not too sweet. The tangor tree grows to 6 feet high and is somewhat wider than a tangor tree on dwarf rootstock.

The key to creating the effect of an orangerie is having the orange trees in matched pots. The Spanish typically use large, rough, sunbaked clay pots. The Italians prefer smooth

kiln-fired terra-cotta pots with bas-relief patterns of garlands or masks, and the French and English use white wooden Versailles tubs with finials at each corner. The pots must be from 18 to 24 inches in diameter, and no less in depth. In a formal orangerie, the trees are all grown to the same height and pruned almost like topiary, into identical rounds, ovals, squares, or columns. Trees that are to be wintered indoors should be on heavy-duty plant trolleys so they can be rolled in and out easily.

A sunny patio of Mexican pavers 20 feet square might be lined on two sides by three 'Robertson' navel orange trees on each side in big, rough Mexican pots incised with stylized medallionlike flowers. A half-dozen trees will produce a great deal of fruit; fortunately, oranges keep well on the tree. Prune the trees to shape when they are in bloom, and bring the branches indoors to create fragrant bouquets. This orangerie will supply your family, friends, and neighbors with an abundance of healthful vitamin C for years. Perhaps that's why oranges symbolize generosity in the traditional language of flowers.

Four different varieties of oranges planted in Versailles tubs would look handsome and smell wonderful on a sunny deck. For this outdoor room, choose 'Washington', 'Valencia', 'Moro', and 'Sanguinelli' trees. Use the fruit of the 'Washington' for eating right off the tree, the 'Valencia' for juice, and the blood oranges of the 'Moro' and 'Sanguinelli' for gourmet treats. The 'Washington' begins bearing in December, the 'Valencia' ripens in summer, 'Moro' from January to April, and 'Sanguinelli' from February to May.

A sleek, modern look can be achieved by planting orange trees in black glazed cylindrical pots. These are dramatic on the terrace of a Los Angeles penthouse or lining the path to the front door of a contemporary house. Mulch the pots with 2 to 3 inches of polished round black river rocks. Use dwarf 'Shamouti' orange trees for the extraordinary beauty of both their leaves and their shape. The trees are wider than they are tall, so they are particularly effective grown in a double row, creating a solid wall from eye level to about 8 feet. In the early spring the trees hang heavy with large, golden, seedless fruit. 'Shamouti' is considered by many to be the finest orange grown, superior even to the commercial 'Washington' navel.

GARDEN RETREATS

Utterly private and perfumed winter and summer, your garden can be a refuge and retreat from all the hustle and bustle of an overburdened, overcommitted life.

The Walled Garden

Create the effect of a medieval walled garden by planting a thick, dense hedge of the sour orange 'Bouquet des Fleurs' around a herringbone brick patio. 'Bouquet des Fleurs' has graceful dark green foliage and extremely large and fragrant flowers. The fruit is small and useful only in bitter marmalade. This hedge is one of the hardiest of the citrus. For privacy, prune the hedge so it is 6 to 8 feet high. Choose appropriate trees and plant them 3 to 4 feet apart on three sides of the patio. Leave room for a 3- to 4-foot-wide arch at the end farthest from the house. (This assumes that one side of the patio attaches to the house; if it does not, hedge all four sides.)

On the arch, plant star-jasmine (*Trachelospermum jasminoides*). Not a true jasmine, star-jasmine is an evergreen vine with glossy leaves and wondrously scented white flowers that bloom in summer. In the center of the garden, place a fountain with a recirculating pump to add privacy and the music of water to the perfumed air.

Place a pair of teak garden benches against the hedge. The benches should face the fountain from opposite sides of the patio. Put a pot with a rosebush in each corner and one at either end of each bench—that's eight pots, enough to have one of each of the old roses listed in the next paragraph.

In large terra-cotta pots, grow a collection of old garden roses. Old garden roses, according to the American Rose Society, are those that were grown before the introduction of tea rose hybrids in 1867. The old garden roses are not only beautiful, but fragrant, disease resistant, and hardy. They require little pruning. Their only drawback is that (except for the Bourbons and hybrid perpetuals) they bloom but once a year. All the heritage roses mentioned in this section are eligible for the American Rose Society's 'Dowager Queen' Award and are among the highest-ranked antique roses. The choicest damask roses include pale pink 'Celsiana' and the green-eyed white 'Madame Hardy'. The finest gallicas include the

deep pink 'Apothecary's Rose', the pink-striped 'Rosa Mundi', and the dark mauve and red 'Tuscany Superb'. The best Bourbon rose is 'Souvenir de la Malmaison'; the best alba rose is the shell-pink 'Maiden's Blush'; the finest hybrid perpetual is the lavender 'Reine des Violettes'; and the choicest moss rose is the mauve 'William Lobb'. The 'Rosa Mundi' and 'Madame Hardy' will tolerate some shade.

The Garden Entwined

Vines are one of the fastest ways to transform a balcony, lanai, arbor, or patio into a bower. Most are fast-growing, many have flowers, and quite a few are fragrant as well. Vines are a particularly felicitous combination of beauty and practicality. They achieve dramatic effects, yet take remarkably little space in the ground and grow successfully in containers where no ground is available. For the amount of foliage and flowers they produce, they require remarkably little water once established.

Technically, a vine is a plant that needs support. Vines have three different ways of climbing: by secreting an adhesive from aerial rootlets, as English ivy (*Hedera helix*) or Virginia creeper (*Parthenocissus quinquefolia*) does; by twining stems around a narrow branch

Top: Walled gardens are a luxury in an urban environment. Vines absorb sound and supply a pleasant view of greenery. Bottom: Seclusion and repose are the hallmarks of the walled garden.

Covered with grape-vines and surrounded by a sedate vegetable garden, an arbor need not be large to furnish a place for escape and contemplation.

or pole support, as honeysuckle (*Lonicera*) does; or by twining tendrils or leaf petioles, as clematis does. It is true that some vines do need a sturdy trellis or arbor to climb on, but a substantial number are self-clinging, which means all you have to do is plant them and get out of their way.

Vines that get huge and heavy, such as wisteria or oriental bittersweet (*Celastrus orbiculatus*), must have substantial support from the day they are planted. When using wood as an arbor or arch, be sure it has been pressure-treated with a wood preservative. Be cautious about growing vines against wooden buildings: The vines hold moisture that can encourage rot. Algerian ivy (*Hedera canariensis*) can happily insinuate itself under the shingles of shingled houses; wisteria is perfectly capable of prying apart wooden railings it has twined around. Honeysuckle can leave deep ridges where it has wrapped itself around a tree. A vine should not have to be pruned back constantly just to keep it within bounds—if it

does, it's in the wrong place. Don't plant a problem: Make certain the vine has adequate support and will not damage or destroy whatever it happens to climb on.

Vines do need pruning to remove dead, diseased, or injured wood, to prevent thatch from building up under the vine, and to encourage flowering. Flowering vines that bloom on new wood are pruned in winter; vines that flower on old wood are pruned when their blooming season ends. Prune deciduous vines during dormancy; trim back extraneous growth in summer when the season's growth is complete. Avoid pruning in the fall because the cuts heal more slowly and new flushes of growth may be killed back by frost. Cut back to the ring from which the branch grows, but do not cut into it; the wound will heal faster.

The Balcony Bower

A balcony can be a real challenge to the gardener, simply because it is so exposed. A high-rise balcony has no trees tall enough to provide protection from wind or shelter from the sun. North-facing balconies tend to be shady and cold; west-facing balconies tend to be baked by afternoon sun. South-facing balconies are typically warm; east-facing balconies enjoy the sunrise and the morning sun. Vines can help to warm cool balconies by deflecting and diminishing the force of the wind and help to cool warm balconies by providing shade and foliage. And, of course, with their flowers and sweet scent, vines can make any balcony prettier and more pleasant.

Vertical gardening is a must on most balconies simply because of their limited space. A long, narrow planter or tall, deep urn is the place to plant a self-clinging vine like creeping fig (*Ficus pumila*) or Boston ivy (*Parthenocissus tricuspidata*). Both will create a delicate pattern up the wall and eventually cover it in a flat mass of vertical green. Creeping fig is evergreen, but Boston ivy turns a spectacular scarlet in the fall. Variegated creeping fig (*F. pumila* 'Variegatus') has dainty, white-edged leaves that are exceptionally attractive.

If you grow bird's-foot ivy (*Hedera helix* 'Pedata') in a narrow planter at the foot of the balcony railing and it twines up each rail, it will eventually drape over the top to form a year-round curtain of dark green. If you want flowers as well as foliage, plant trumpetcreeper

(*Campsis radicans*), a dense woody vine that has deep-orange hummingbird-attracting flowers in summer and fall. It blooms on new wood, so trim the vine back in early spring to have lots of flowers. The trumpetcreeper is a northeastern native hardy to zone 4. Brown's honeysuckle (*Lonicera × brownii* 'Dropmore Scarlet') has a profusion of red flowers from June through late fall. It too attracts hummingbirds and is hardy as far north as zone 3.

For a flamboyant mass of flowers and foliage, plant morning glories, fast-growing vines with attractive heart-shaped leaves. They are used as annuals in cold-winter climates but are often evergreen in warm-winter areas. For a fabulous display, plant more than one variety. (Nick the seeds with a knife and soak them overnight to hasten germination.) Combine imperial Japanese morning glory (*Ipomoea nil*) with 'Heavenly Blue' morning glory (*I. tricolor*) and white moonflower (*I. alba*). The imperial Japanese morning glory comes in a wide variety of cultivars that may be violet, purple, blue, rose, or multicolored and in shapes that are fluted, fringed, or double. A combination of a fringed or fluted rose might be lovely combined with sky-colored 'Heavenly Blue' and the huge white moonflower. Most morning glories open in the morning and fade by afternoon; moonflower has white, fragrant flowers that bloom at night. For the price of a half-dozen seeds, these three morning glories put on a tremendous show from early morning on through the long summer nights. In cold climates, the morning glories must be pulled in the late fall, leaving the railing bare for the winter, but who will be on the balcony in a blizzard anyway?

A combination of perennial clematis can put on a show as dramatic as that of the morning glories. In cold climates, combine rich purple Jackman clematis (*Clematis × jackmanii*) with golden clematis (*C. tangutica*), which has masses of bright yellow bell-shaped flowers. Both are hardy to zone 3 and will bloom separately and together. The Jackman blooms heavily from June or July until frost. The golden clematis blooms in June, intermittently through the summer, and profusely again in late summer and fall. In warmer climates, combine the evergreen Armand clematis (*C. armandii*) with anemone clematis (*C. montana*) and sweet autumn clematis (*C. maximowicziana*). The result will be billowy masses of delicately scented white flowers from early spring all through the summer into fall.

If you want foliage, flowers, and stop-in-your-tracks fragrance, grow star-jasmine, everblooming honeysuckle (*Lonicera × heckrotti*), poet's-jasmine (*Jasminum officinale* 'Grandiflorum'), or sweet peas (*Lathyrus odoratus*) up the railing.

If you want foliage, flowers, fragrance, and food, grow passionfruit (*Passiflora edulis*), with its strange white and purple flowers and fragrant purple fruit. *Passiflora edulis* 'Incense'—which has 5-inch flowers that smell

Left: A single vine correctly placed adds interest to what would otherwise be a mundane exterior. Right: Any city dweller with an outdoor space, no matter how cramped, can enjoy a wall fountain. They come in various styles and sizes and can be purchased at many garden centers.

Top: Most clematis are well behaved and can be allowed to climb as they will.
Center: Different species of honeysuckle (Lonicera) *have different growth characteristics. For a small patio or balcony, choose a non-invasive variety.*
Bottom: Espaliered dwarf fruit trees are perfect for balconies. This apricot tree is as arresting in winter as it is in summer.

like sweet peas, and yellow-green edible fruit—is hardy to 0° F. Maypop (*P. incarnata*), a very hardy native of the eastern United States, has 2-inch white and purple flowers and edible yellowish fruit.

Passionflowers attract orange and black gulf fritillary butterflies (*Agraulis vanillae*), which are a delight to watch. Unfortunately, their alter egos—handsome black-spined red-striped caterpillars—consider passionflowers a gourmet delight, so pick the caterpillars off should they put in an appearance. Gulf fritillary caterpillars are easy to raise in captivity. Watch a black caterpillar turn into a brown chrysalis and then an orange butterfly that will fly hundreds of miles back to the tropics, and you will see a miracle with your own eyes.

Because they're vigorous, passionflowers need to be pruned annually after the second year to keep thatch from building up. Cut excess branches back to the base or to the juncture with another branch.

With hummingbirds or butterflies, walls of green, and the railing a burst of bloom from spring into summer, the next addition to this urban balcony bower should be a hanging basket or two of impatiens or tuberous begonias. Add a comfortable wicker chair with plump chintz pillows and a long, tall lemonade to sustain you while you observe hummingbird or butterfly behavior. Your neighbors may want to give you an urban good-neighbor award because of the beauty and fragrance your garden brings to the neighborhood.

Vines can transform decks as effectively as balconies. Simply think of the deck railing as a built-in trellis and go from there. Climbing roses can be tied to the tops of railings with plant ties or green string. They can also be laced through the railings or trellised up walls. Even with no space but the deck, it's possible to have a flourishing rose garden.

There are some tremendous advantages to growing roses in containers. Poor soil is not a problem, since you can simply use potting mix. It's easier to fertilize a dozen pots of rosebushes than rosebushes scattered around the garden. Pests and diseases are easier to control because the roses are easier to spray when they're in a relatively compact space. And deer are less likely to prowl the deck at night than the garden.

Climbing roses trained (usually tied) horizontally, such as along a deck railing, bloom

more abundantly than roses trained to grow upward. Climbing roses need at least six hours of sun a day to bloom well. They need large pots, at least 14 inches in diameter and at least 12 inches deep. Tall amphoras work wonderfully well because they're so deep.

On a small deck, use one of the miniature climbing roses, either pink 'Little Girl' or light-red 'Hi-Ho'. 'Little Girl' has canes 4 to 5 feet long; 'Hi-Ho' has canes 6 to 7 feet long. On a larger deck, plant former All-American Rose Selection winner 'Golden Showers', a magnificent daffodil-yellow rose that blooms abundantly and is fragrant as well. Trellis its canes against a wall, since it is inclined to be upright from 8 to 10 feet. The canes grow to 15 feet, but they can simply lie on the roof as roses habitually do on summer cottages in Siasconset on Nantucket. If you have a long railing (at least 20 feet), grow the nearly thornless, highly disease-resistant old garden rose Lady Banks' Rose (*Rosa banksiae* 'Alba Plena'), an evergreen climber with double, white, violet-scented roses that flower from spring through midsummer. Other good candidates for a long railing are these climbers: light pink sweetheart rose 'Cécile Brünner'; blush pink 'New Dawn'; and the very fragrant, very hardy, deep-pink 'Viking Queen'.

In large, deep pots grow a small collection of classic roses. The damask rose 'York and Lancaster' has some flowers that are pink, some that are white, and some that are pink and white. Damask roses are very fragrant, loosely double, and grow in clusters. An excellent alba rose (*R. alba*) introduced in 1826 is 'Konigin von Danemark' ('Queen of Denmark'), which British rose authority Graham Thomas calls "a jewel beyond price." With a deep pink flower that fades to pale pink and is intensely fragrant, the 'Konigin von Danemark' grows to 5 feet and blooms freely. The floribunda 'Gruss an Aachen' is a superb small rose introduced in 1909. It grows 2 feet tall and 3 feet wide and flowers readily in shade. The blossoms grow in natural bouquets of salmon pink, and it blooms over a long period. Another excellent small rose is the centifolia 'Rose de Meaux', which also produces sweetly fragrant pink flowers on a bush only 2 feet tall.

Ten or twelve of these roses—all in pots, some trained along a sunny railing, some trellised up the wall, some freestanding—combine

A rose lover need not be limited by lack of room. This 'Coral Dawn' climbs a gazebo arbor.

to make a lovely garden of choice roses to view from the house or to cut for the house.

The Shady Arbor

Many patios have sturdy arbors built to help shade and cool the patio in summer, and arbors are one of the places vines really shine. Plant a Chinese wisteria (*W. sinensis*) next to a sturdy post, and tie the stems where you want them to grow. (Be sure to use wisteria grown from a cutting; wisteria takes forever from seed and grafted plants can sprout below the graft.) Wisteria is extremely long-lived, and the main stem eventually develops a thick trunk worthy of a tree. It needs to be well watered and well fed when it's young and pretty much left alone once it's reached blooming size: Mature wisteria flowers better with minimal food and water. In the winter, prune flowering shoots and thin outside shoots, leaving only two or three fat flower buds. In the summer, cut back any loose streamers, preserving only those you want to tie up over the arbor. If this seems like a lot of trouble, rest assured that wisteria is more than worth the effort. Wisteria blooms in long, lightly scented, violet-blue clusters in April and May, and it is nothing short of spectacular. The leaves provide a cool, green shade all summer and turn a clear yellow in fall.

Place a garden arch in the center of each of the three sides of the patio that adjoin the garden. At the bases of the arches, plant flowering vines. In keeping with the blue-violet color scheme suggested by the wisteria, plant rich *Clematis* × *jackmanii* on one arch (two plants to each arch, one on either side); lavender-blue

C. montana 'Ramona' on the second; and the old-fashioned indigo C. × *durandii*, introduced in France in 1870, to bloom the summer through on the third arch. Clematis are unusual in that they are lovely when they are past bloom: The flowers leave behind feathery silvery seed heads that are almost as ornamental as the flowers themselves.

At the edges of the patio, on all three sides from the corners to the arches, plant a border of bear's-breech (*Acanthus mollis*). Its big, glossy, dark-green leaves are so beautiful that the Greeks chiseled their shape into marble to decorate the pediments of columns and the friezes of temples. The flower spikes are tall, striking, and strange, blooming in late spring or early summer. Sink a metal barrier—3 feet of metal flashing—to confine the roots, or bear's-breech will expand across the lawn.

If there is a border between the house and patio, plant climbing hydrangea (*Hydrangea anomala* ssp. *petiolaris*) in the ground so it

can climb on the wall of the house. Plant it in large tubs if no ground is available. Climbing hydrangea is self-clinging; has fragrant, white lace-cap flowers in June and July; rich green foliage; and exfoliating bark for winter interest. Trim it to size each year, or let it round the corners of the house and cling where it will: Climbing hydrangea can cover up to 80 feet at maturity. Imagine a house with walls completely covered in flowers two months of the year! It's a perfectly splendid way to render unattractive or undistinguished architecture irrelevant.

Even the plainest concrete-slab patio would become a pleasant and peaceful refuge with wisteria overhead, the three arches covered with flowers doing variations on a theme of the blues, and a wall of white hydrangea to scent the arbor's summer shade. Furnished with a big teak or redwood table, a pair of benches, and a barbecue in an unobtrusive corner, this might be the setting for a delightful picnic or the favorite place to eat dinner all summer long.

The Perfumed Garden

A half-barrel of fragrance can evoke echoes of a Moorish courtyard. Picture a rosebush noted for its fragrance encircled by a neatly clipped hedge of dwarf myrtle (*Myrtus communis* 'Compacta'). Old roses noted for their fragrance include the apothecary's rose, or Red Rose of Lancaster (*Rosa gallica* 'Officinalis'); the White Rose of York (*R. alba* 'Semi Plena') and another alba rose, 'Félicité Parmentier'; the damask rose 'La Ville de Bruxelles'; the compact centifolia 'Rose de Meaux'; the moss rose, 'Muscosa Alba', also known as 'Shailer's White Moss'; and the Bourbon roses 'Louise Odier' and 'Madame Pierre Oger'. Heritage roses, once established, require far less deadheading, pruning, fertilizing, watering, and spraying than modern hybrids, but modern hybrids are more readily available. Sweetly scented hybrid roses include the New England rose 'Heritage' and the tea roses 'Tiffany' and 'Fragrant Cloud'.

Citrus can be the keynote of a garden of fragrance on any terrace or patio that gets full sun. In a large bas-relief Italian pot in the center of the patio, plant the intriguing 'Sungold' lemon tree. Its leaves are mottled with cream and white, its yellow fruit striped with green. 'Sungold' grows to 14 feet tall and 8 feet wide. At the corners of the patio, in matching pots, plant a 'Kinnow' tangerine, a 'Minneola' tangelo, a 'Moro' blood orange, and a 'Temple' tangor. Underplant the trees with Corsican mint to create a fragrant living mulch. This collection of exotic citrus provides flowers, fragrance, and fruit from December through spring.

Pots of formally clipped English lavender (*Lavandula officinalis*), bay laurel (*Laurus nobilis*), sweet myrtle (*Myrtus communis*), and rosemary (*Rosmarinus officinalis*) would scent the summer and give the outdoor room the feel and fragrance of a Mediterranean villa.

This is primarily a green garden—cool, quiet, and serene. For more color and fragrance, trellis the antique roses 'Celsiana' and 'Petite de Holland' up the walls of the house. The pale pink 'Celsiana' is a damask rose; it has a long midseason blooming period and is neat and attractive when out of bloom. 'Petite de Holland' is a Provence rose and widely considered to be the best centifolia for small gardens. Centifolia roses are also known as cabbage roses. 'Petite de Holland' has very fragrant medium-pink flowers, and like 'Celsiana', it is hardy. In pots bank-

Top: Phlox (Phlox paniculata) *fills this front porch with the scent of summer. Bottom: The fragrant dwarf myrtle* (Myrtus communis 'Compacta') *fits into any nook.*

ing the roses, plant white madonna lilies for still more summer bloom and fragrance.

Furnish this outdoor room with a French bistro table and matching chairs or a pair of teak steamer chairs and intricately patterned Provençal pillows. The sweet perfume of citrus through the winter; the scent of roses, lilies, and sweet herbs in the summer; fruit to pluck off the trees; and shade to sit in—this garden is what relaxation is all about.

MINIATURE SANCTUARIES FOR BIRDS

A paved cityscape seems an unlikely bird habitat. The birds that live in such an environment depend for survival on oases of greenery. By providing the resources birds need, you can improve their quality of life and your own. Invite birds into your outdoor room and enjoy their colors, songs, and antics.

Bird Feeders

Feeding stations come in several specialized forms. There are nectar feeders for hummingbirds and orioles; seed feeders for warblers, finches, blue jays, and cardinals; suet feeders for chickadees and woodpeckers; and fruit feeders for orioles, jays, and other fruit-eating birds.

Seed dispensers   To keep scattered seed from making a mess on the deck, hang seed-filled feeders from a tree close to the deck or patio. Put different kinds of seed in each feeder to attract a variety of birds: thistleseed for goldfinches, sunflower seeds for purple finches, and millet for dark-eyed juncos, for example.

Nectar-filled feeders   Hang nectar-filled feeders from the eaves of the house, so you can watch the birds from a window as well as from the deck. Be sure to get the kind of feeders that don't drip; spilled sugar-water nectar makes a sticky mess and attracts bees and

wasps. The Droll Yankee company makes an excellent dripless hummingbird feeder, shaped rather like a spaceship. The nectar formula, by the way, is 4 parts water to 1 part granulated sugar—or phrased another way, 1 cup sugar to 4 cups water. Sugar water stores perfectly well in the refrigerator if you prefer to make up a big batch in a closed pitcher and keep it ready so you can refill the feeders as soon as they are emptied. Coloring the nectar with red food coloring isn't necessary, since most feeders have red on them already; what attracts the hummingbirds is the scent of the nectar, not its color. Don't use honey to make nectar; it can promote a fungal growth that can kill hummingbirds.

Though hummers are the most renowned fans of sugar-water nectar, other birds readily help themselves to it. Your nectar feeder is likely to attract orioles, chickadees, and the colorful warblers that Roger Tory Peterson calls "the butterflies of the bird world."

Bird-Friendly Plantings

If your outdoor room has space for a half-barrel, you have all the room you need to give hummingbirds a rousing welcome. Consider planting a half-barrel with cardinal flower, foxglove, impatiens, and Russell Hybrids of lupine. The soil in this container must stay fairly moist. Hummingbirds would also show avid interest in a half-barrel containing hollyhock, beebalm,

Left: A bird feeder welcomes feathered garden visitors year-round, providing color and vitality—even in the dead of winter. Right: Hummingbirds may be the best loved of all birds. If you want them to keep calling, add a feeder in addition to the plants that attract them.

blazing-star, and petunia. The soil in this container must stay fairly dry. A genuinely drought-tolerant hummingbird half-barrel contains red-hot-poker, lantana, and trailing nasturtium. These three containers of flowers will provide bloom from spring through summer. Other plants that attract hummingbirds are abelia, flowering quince (*Chaenomeles* spp.), hibiscus, hummingbird bush (*Grevillea thelemanniana*), and weigela. A trellis of goldflame (ever-blooming) honeysuckle (*Lonicera × heckrotti*) attracts hummingbirds during the summer.

A fence or wall covered with Algerian ivy (*Hedera canariensis*) encourages many different kinds of birds to nest and to eat its black berries: These birds include song sparrows, hermit thrushes, and blue jays, to name a few.

A firethorn espaliered against the house can attract flocks of robins who may well become intoxicated and giddy by eating the berries. The holly *Ilex* 'Sparkleberry' provides stupendous amounts of shiny red berries for birds to feed on through the winter. 'Sparkleberry' should be planted with its pollinator, *Ilex* 'Apollo'. When the bushes are young, they can grow in large tubs. When they grow too large for tubs, move them to the foundation border, against the house. Cotoneasters also have bright red berries that are attractive to hummingbirds as well as songbirds.

Small trees that attract hummingbirds include the naturally dwarf Pink Princess™ flow-ering-crab (*Malus* 'Parrsi'), which grows about 8 feet tall; dwarf citrus, which grows up to 10 feet; and chastetree (*Vitex agnus-castus*), which grows to 6 feet in the Pacific Northwest, to 9 feet in zones 6 and 7, and to 25 feet in the low desert.

The design that follows, An Urban Oasis, offers plants to delight the palettes of birds and the eyes of people, and furnishings to make all the inhabitants comfortable.

An Urban Oasis

Grow Boston ivy (*Parthenocissus tricuspidata*) up the sunny back wall of a brownstone, where the foliage will provide shelter and the berries will provide food for birds. In the fall, Boston ivy turns flaming scarlet; in the winter, the vine makes an interesting pattern on a wall. On a sturdy back fence, plant porcelain ampelopsis (*Ampelopsis brevipedunculata*). It has handsomely textured leaves and clusters of berries that start out greenish ivory and turn green, purple, or pink before finally settling on metallic porcelain blue. Its leaves color red in the fall, like the Boston ivy. Over a solidly built pergola, grow crimson glory-vine (*Vitis coignetiae*), which has clusters of tiny grapes that birds adore. It is very fast-growing (as are Boston ivy and porcelain ampelopsis), and its foot-long leaves turn bright crimson in the autumn. Of the three, only the crimson glory-vine needs annual pruning. Not only would these

Left: Cardinal flower (Lobelia cardinalis) attracts hummingbirds. Right: Any patch of calm and repose in the midst of city bustle will draw birds.

If neighborhood cats are not a problem, a simple pedestal birdbath is a pleasant addition beneath a tree.

To create a simple birdbath, fill a 12-inch clay saucer with 2 to 3 inches of water. Set the saucer on a railing or pedestal and make sure it sits securely. Use chains to hang a similar birdbath, glazed on the inside so it won't drip, from the eaves of the house or the branch of a nearby tree. If it is hung from the eaves, be sure a gust of wind won't bang it against the glass of a window. Terra-cotta and concrete birdbaths must be drained before the first freeze, to prevent cracking. Specialty stores and catalogs for bird lovers offer devices to keep birdbath water from freezing so water is available to birds such as cardinals and chickadees, who stay through the winter.

Furnish the pergola with aluminum reproductions of Victorian cast-iron lawn furniture. A white curlicued table and chairs, a lacy tablecloth, an old-fashioned silver teapot, a pair of china teacups, and a plate of Proust's madeleines set the scene for an al fresco afternoon tea in the garden. Tea will be accompanied by live music, provided free by scores of sweetly singing birds.

HANGING GARDENS

The Hanging Gardens of Babylon, created by the wise and powerful Queen Semiramis, bloomed with 300,000 plants. It was considered one of the Seven Wonders of the World. Just the logistics of keeping all the plants in the garden watered must have been enough to qualify it as a wonder. The mechanics notwithstanding, Semiramis knew that hanging baskets can create a garden of stunning magnificence.

The biggest concern with hanging baskets is providing sufficient water. In summer they may need watering several times a week and, during a heat wave, daily. A watering wand may do the job, if water dripping on the deck or balcony is not a concern. A tidier way to go about things is to dunk each basket in a bucket or washtub of water, as described on page 36.

To feed plants in hanging baskets, add soluble fertilizer to the water. Another method is to add a small amount of a slow-release fertilizer to the soil when the plant is potted up. Slow-release fertilizers are round coated pellets that release small amounts of nutrients each time the basket is watered.

Top: A fountain is always a delightful garden accessory. Outdoor creatures find running water as enticing as humans do. Bottom: The beauty of Boston ivy (Parthenocissus tricuspidata) in its fall colors may outweigh its somewhat destructive properties.

three vines attract many songbirds to feed and nest, but they would make the garden feel green and cool in the summer and go out in a blaze of glory in the fall.

If there is room for a tree, plant a Washington hawthorn (*Crataegus phaenopyrum*), a beautiful small tree with glossy leaves, clusters of white flowers in the spring, bright red fruit for the birds to eat on their way south, and scarlet-to-orange color in the autumn. From the tree, hang a birdbath where the birds can drink and bathe without fear of skulking cats.

Plastic containers are good for hanging—they are lightweight; they keep soil moist by reducing moisture loss from evaporation; and they do not chip, crack, or break when bumped or dropped. Use them with plants that will eventually obscure the containers, since they aren't usually particularly attractive.

Wire baskets lined with sphagnum moss are lightweight, unbreakable, and more attractive than plastic pots, but they are likely to dry out faster. Wire baskets are traditional with squirrel's-foot ferns (*Davallia trichomanoides*), because seeing the soft, furry rhizomes is part of the basket's charm.

In potting a hanging basket, leave at least ½ inch—preferably, a full inch—for watering space, especially if you intend to do overhead watering. The ideal is to be able to wet the soil thoroughly in one application.

Hanging baskets need regular grooming to keep them in display condition. Dead leaves and spent blooms need to be trimmed off. Stray shoots need to be cut back or pinned with hairpins to the soil or moss. Plants that poke people in the eye or trail in their coffee are not welcome on the well-managed balcony or lanai.

If a hanging plant will not overwinter in a greenhouse, toss out the plant and the soil and salvage the basket, the hanger, and the sphagnum moss. Store them in the potting shed or garage, to use with new plants next spring. Before replanting pots or baskets, run them through the dishwasher to sterilize them, or dip them in a solution of 1 cup bleach to 1 gallon water and rinse them well. Pouring boiling water over sphagnum moss not only sterilizes it, but also makes it easier to work with. Give it plenty of time to cool off before handling it; sphagnum holds heat a surprisingly long while. Sterilizing pots and moss prevents any overwintering pests or diseases from cutting down your freshly potted plants in their early youth.

Wire baskets are excellent for planting mixed bouquets of flowers—for example, white evergreen candytuft, yellow basket-of-gold, and purple aubrietia, or blue trailing lobelia, white Italian bellflower, and blue Kenilworth ivy. A mixed bouquet works best when all the plants in it have the same requirements for light and water. Leave the requisite inch at the top for watering, and add slow-release fertilizer in the top inch of soil, if that's how you decide to feed the bouquet. Soak the basket thoroughly, and let it drain before hanging it.

Carefully choose the place to hang a basket. Be sure it won't be whacked every time some-

A few hanging plants of the right form and color create an eye-catching display.

body opens the door or window. Make certain it is hung high enough that tall people don't bump their heads. Most important, be absolutely positive that the hook is secure (see Suspending Planters Safely, in the third chapter). Falling not only wrecks the plants, but it creates an extremely awkward social situation if the planter hits someone on its way down.

Hanging baskets are not the only way to enjoy a hanging garden. The section called Plants That Hang, in the second chapter, discusses window boxes, planter frames, and trellises. Molded terra-cotta planters come in the form of masks, lion heads, and other fanciful shapes that need only to be planted and hung on an outside wall.

It's essential to be careful in choosing which plants to grow. Some grow well in shade, others do better with at least morning or afternoon sun, and some need sun most of the day. Oddly enough, the most flamboyant bloomers all prefer filtered shade: fuchsias, tuberous begonias, orchid cactuses (*Epiphyllum chrysocardium*), achimenes, and impatiens. Foliage plants that do well in filtered shade include donkey's-tail (*Sedum morganianum*), bear's-foot fern (*Humata tyermannii*), Boston fern (*Nephrolepsis exaltata* 'Bostoniensis'), hare's-foot fern

(*Polypodium aureum*), lettuce-fern (*P. aureum* 'Mandaianum'), and squirrel's-foot fern (*Davallia trichomanoides*). Plants for half-day sun are asparagus fern (*Asparagus densiflorus* 'Sprengeri'), English ivy (*Hedera helix*), ivy geranium (*Pelargonium peltatum*), trailing lobelia (*Lobelia erinus*), Italian bellflower (*Campanula isophylla*), Kenilworth ivy (*Cymbalaria muralis*), dwarf periwinkle (*Vinca minor*), and moneywort (*Lysimachia nummularia*). For areas that get sun most of the day, use aubrieta (*Aubrieta deltoidea*), basket-of-gold (*Aurinia saxatilis*), bearberry cotoneaster (*Cotoneaster dammeri*), evergreen candytuft (*Iberis sempervirens*), cascade petunia (*Petunia × hybrida* 'Supercascade'), euonymus (*Euonymus fortunei* 'Gracilis'), shore juniper (*Juniperus conferta* 'Emerald Sea'), 'Improved Sweet 100' tomato, lantana (*Lantana montevidensis*), and parrotbeak (*Clianthus puniceus*).

The Summer Verandah

An old-fashioned verandah that curves around the outside of a summer cottage is the perfect place to grow hanging plants. Hanging baskets with lush foliage and exquisite flowers are not only magnificent in an outdoor room, but they are splendid viewed from inside the house as

Left: Hanging plants are ideal when the ground must be clear of obstacles.
Right: Periwinkle (Vinca minor) *makes an ideal hanging plant. Keep it compact or let it trail.*

well. On the north side of the verandah, hang a half-dozen well-grown pots of Boston fern, and hang among them another half-dozen wire baskets of white impatiens. On the east side, hang baskets of trailing 'Needlepoint' English ivy and white ivy geranium. On the west side, put up pots of variegated white petunia—*Euonymus fortunei* 'Gracilis' and 'Cascade'.

Furnish this lushly landscaped verandah with old-fashioned white wicker furniture: a big round dining table and chairs, a chaise lounge or turn-of-the-century daybed, and a few big, comfortable chairs complete with fat chintz pillows to laze away the day on. Finish the look with a white wicker fern stand with an immense 'Fluffy Ruffles' Boston fern or wicker planters filled with pots of asparagus fern.

This summer verandah speaks eloquently of the quiet luxury of the turn of the century, when leisure meant curling up with a good romance and reading without interruption. Such a verandah was the place where a small child came to crawl sleepily into a welcoming lap. On a hot afternoon, a verandah is a cool place to serve fresh lemonade poured over crushed ice, each tall glass garnished with a sprig of mint. And, as the long summer evening gently eases to its close, it is the place to serve homemade peach ice cream.

The Mediterranean Arcade

Mediterranean-style houses sometimes have a covered arcade along the front. The floor is tiled, and stucco or adobe arches let shafts of sunlight penetrate into the shaded corridor. Trellis *Bougainvillea* 'San Diego Red' or 'Scarlett O'Hara' on each pillar. Let it grow as high as the eaves, and train it on wire over the arches. In the center of each arch, hang a pot of bright yellow lantana 'Spreading Sunshine' or basket-of-gold. Inside the arcade, suspend pots of donkey's-tail very high, so the foliage can trail. On the inside of the pillars, hang black wrought-iron wall brackets. Into the brackets slip pots of white orchid cactus. Position the brackets so that the large, exotic flowers, some as large as 10 inches across, are at eye level, where they can be fully appreciated. Orchid cactus blooms April through June. When the cactuses are finished blooming, replace them with pots of summer- and fall-blooming tuberous begonias. Against the wall opposite each arch, place tall Spanish urns planted with

Top: When landscaping a long passage, pathway, or stairway, use one type of plant to lead the eye from beginning to end. Bottom: Comfortably furnished verandahs awaken the desire to sit and read or converse with passing neighbors.

choice lady palms (*Rhapis excelsa*) 5 feet tall. At one end of the corridor, install a wall fountain with a fluted basin and recirculating pump.

In this arcade, relax in Mexican barrel chairs on a sultry afternoon while a light breeze plays through the arches. Late in the evening, while watching a summer sunset perhaps, serve *tapas*, delectable Spanish hors d'oeuvres, on a weather-beaten manzanita table. And if some of the orchid cactuses are of the night-blooming variety, you might have a special party to watch the orchids open.

Wire holders can support pots or window boxes on the outside of a railing. Be sure containers are securely fastened and can take the weight you intend to place in them.

The Babylonian Balcony

A small balcony is probably the most challenging place in which to garden, since everything must be planted in containers and floor space is limited. The solution is a hanging garden to rival that of ancient Babylon. In the darkest corner, suspend one spectacular hanging basket of pink and white fuchsia. Use French wire holders to hang pots of pale pink ivy geraniums or pink cascade petunias from the railing. If the balcony has a window, put in a window box planted with masses of pale pink and white impatiens.

If your balcony looks out over a river or garden or gets the sunset every evening, frame the view with large hanging pots of asparagus fern. Should the balcony look directly into high-rise walls or straight at the next building's fire escape, block the view with a series of hanging pots trailing the variegated English ivy 'Glacier'. The gently swaying curtain of almost-white ivy blocks uninspiring views and gives the balcony substantially more privacy.

On one end wall, hang a terra-cotta planter in the shape of a lion's head and give it a green mane of Kenilworth ivy. On the opposite wall, install a spouting lion's-head fountain and let the sound of water help soothe away the sounds of traffic and neighbors. A tall maharaja chair and a small table to hold a glass and a book finish this green aerie off nicely. This is a tranquil place to come home to after a long day at work and a delightful place to sling a Yucatan hammock from the ceiling and sleep outdoors on summer nights.

ORIENTAL INFLUENCES

Both Japanese and Chinese gardens are designed according to symbolism and spiritual principles thousands of years old. A simple five-part stone lantern may symbolize the five elements of the ancient Japanese cosmology—sky, wind, fire, water, and earth. Another stone lantern may symbolize the earth, heaven, and humanity by incorporating a rectangle at the base, a triangle at the top, and a circle in the middle. The Chinese philosopher-poet Lao-tsu postulated the principle of opposites: the yin and the yang, the masculine and the feminine, the light and the dark, the negative and the positive. The rugged rocks so essential to Japanese garden design are considered to be no less alive than the plants; it is important to recognize their "faces" and acknowledge their "spirits."

Asymmetry is the cornerstone of Japanese garden design, because nature is perceived as being asymmetrical. Trees are never paired, one planting is not balanced with a mirror image. Paths are never absolutely straight and never lead directly to a destination: They wind and wander, each curve revealing a new view, a different perspective. A group of trees intended to suggest a forest or grove always contains an uneven number of trees. Three is a highly symbolic number, and plants are often grouped in threes.

Japanese and Chinese gardens use many plants that flower, but the plants are not usually grown for their flowers. A group of azaleas may be pruned in rounded shapes to evoke the image of rounded hills. If flowers are sacrificed in the process, so be it. The shape and symbolism take precedence. Japanese gardens are often essentially evergreen gardens, featuring evergreen trees and shrubs such as pines, azaleas, Japanese andromedas (*Pieris*), and camellias (*C. sasanqua*). Having said that, it is true that the Japanese garden calendar is largely a calendar of bloom and fall color, featuring each species in its season, each species at its greatest beauty: January features pine; February, plum; March, peach and pear; April, cherry; May, azalea, peony, and wisteria; June, iris; July, morning glory; August, lotus; September, the seven grasses of autumn; October, chrysanthemum; November, maple; December, camellia.

To create a patio or deck or balcony to delight the eye and keep alive the hope that spring will one day come again, consider a simple oriental garden.

A Contemplation Garden

Lay a curved rough stone patio and plant moss between the stones. Edge the curve with low-growing evergreen kurume *Rhododendron* 'Snow' azaleas trimmed into flowing mounds like a ridge of rounded hills. In five cobalt-blue Malaysian pickle pots, grow camellias. Two excellent *Camellia japonica* are the large, formal white formal double 'Alba Plena', which was brought from China in 1792, and the large, white anemone-flowered 'Shiro Chan', itself well over 100 years old. Where rains may damage the flowers of the early-blooming 'Alba Plena', choose instead the very large white, peony-flowered 'Swan Lake', which blooms midseason to late season. (In California, early is October through January, midseason is January to March, and late is March through May. In the Pacific Northwest, early bloom starts in January, midseason comes in March, and late season is in May. Ask at your local nursery to learn how the terms translate in your region.) The 'Alba Plena' blooms early; 'Shiro Chan' blooms midseason. *C. japonica* does best in filtered shade or morning sun, but *C. sasanqua* will tolerate much more sun, even full sun, given sufficient moisture. 'Hana Jiman', with white semidouble flowers edged with pink; 'Mine-No-Yuki' ('White Doves'), a white peony-form double; and 'Setsugekka', with large white

semidouble flowers and fluted petals, are all choice selections. All of these bloom in fall and early winter. Make a loose grouping of the five camellias, the more upright, bushy *C. japonica* providing an evergreen background for the graceful, almost willowy *C. sasanqua*.

In a tall dark brown Chinese ginger pot, grow Japanese andromeda (lily-of-the-valley shrub) or *Pieris japonica* 'Mountain Fire' or 'Spring Snow'. 'Mountain Fire' can eventually grow to 10 feet, but it is best pruned to emphasize its naturally tiered form and to keep it somewhat lower. Its new growth, far more dramatic than its dainty little flowers, is flame red, and pruning encourages new growth. 'Spring Snow' is more compact, growing to between 3 and 6 feet, and it carries its flower clusters upright. Its new growth is not as striking as that of 'Mountain Fire', however.

In a Chinese egg jar (which is also called a dragon pot), plant a tall fern pine (*Podocarpus gracilior*). Although fern pines can eventually reach 60 feet, they grow slowly, with great dignity and grace, and will thrive for many years in a container—especially one as large as an egg jar.

At the edge of the patio, put in a weeping flowering cherry tree (*Prunus subhirtella* 'Pendula'). Place it close enough to the patio that the weeping branches, ethereal with pink

Left: The placement of plants and materials, not necessarily their species or type, is what produces a garden with a Japanese ambience. You can use American species and still create the effect.
Right: Stone lanterns are a hallmark of Japanese gardens. When combined with Golden Goddess bamboo (Bambusa multiplex 'Golden Goddess') or a specially trimmed azalea, they add an Asian accent to any garden.

blossoms, will eventually sweep across the stones and moss. Allow branches to grow until they trail to the ground, suggesting a ballerina bending to the floor. Weeping cherries should be pruned as little as possible. Trim them while they bloom, to remove any crossing or stubbornly upright branches, and use the flowering branches in arrangements. (Broken, diseased, or dead wood should always be removed post-haste.)

One specimen, red laceleaf maple (*Acer palmatum* var. *dissectum* 'Ornatum'), should complete the collection of trees. To show off this extraordinary tree, give it the place of honor, an eye-stopping point of display, and a self-effacing pot. Red laceleaf maples are exquisite in every season of the year. Winter reveals the gracefully draping, tiered branches; spring unfolds pink leaves that darken to red; summer shows the delicately cut leaves on arching branches in all their glory; and in fall

Top: You need only a single bonsai tree in a carefully chosen setting to create a notable arrangement. Podocarpus *make particularly striking bonsai. Bottom left: Wherever they are planted, weeping cherry trees evoke a feeling of spring in Japan. Bottom right: Black pine* (Pinus thunbergiana) *make excellent bonsai specimens.*

the leaves color from burgundy to scarlet. It is an altogether satisfying tree.

No oriental garden is complete without bamboo, and the best for container growing are Golden Goddess bamboo (*Bambusa multiplex* 'Golden Goddess') and Chinese Goddess bamboo (*Bambusa multiplex* var. *rivierorum*). Golden Goddess grows to 10 feet but can be kept to between 6 and 8 feet; Chinese Goddess grows to 8 feet but can be kept to between 4 and 6 feet. Both are graceful, arching grasses, and Chinese Goddess is notable for its small, lacy, fernlike sprays of leaves. Combine these with sacred bamboo (*Nandina domestica* 'Umpqua Chief'), which grows to 6 feet but can easily be kept to 3 feet by simply pruning out the oldest canes. Sacred bamboo echoes the seasonal progression of the red laceleaf maple. The new leaves are pink and reddish-bronze. They turn a soft, pale green as they mature, coloring fiery crimson in the fall. Airy sprays of white flowers bloom in the summer and, if several sacred bamboo plants are placed together, they will bear shiny red berries all through winter. A handsome grouping would consist of three sacred bamboo backed by one Golden Goddess bamboo and one Chinese bamboo.

In the fall, include pots of spider or decorative chrysanthemums. Spider mums have long, curling, tubular petals (rays) with ends curved like fishhooks; decorative mums, which have overlapping, 'shingled' petals, are the stylized chrysanthemums so often seen in Japanese art.

A single large bonsai of a Japanese black pine growing out of moss would be the finishing horticultural touch on this mossy, stone patio inspired by the temple gardens of the Ori-

When you display bonsai in a natural setting, remember to include spots from which to view them.

ent. Near the bonsai or the maple, place a carefully chosen rugged rock or a stone water basin to contrast with the smooth glazes of the ceramic pots. Japanese nurseries carry stone basins; building-supply yards sell rocks. Wander around looking until one catches your eye, until you can see its face and recognize its spirit. Have the supplier deliver and position the rock for you.

In a large peony-flowered oriental ceramic fishbowl, plant a pot of orchid iris (*Iris japonica*). Orchid iris are considered the most beautiful of the crested iris, blooming with fringed pale lavender flowers in late spring. Then add two golden koi (*Cyprinus carpio*). If cats or raccoons are likely nocturnal prowlers and predators, cut wire hardware cloth to size and bend it into place an inch or so under the water. The predators can't get in, and the orchid iris can easily grow out through the mesh. The koi vendor will explain how to keep the fish healthy and happy.

This entire garden can be brought indoors for the winter. The bamboos, camellias, fern pine, and irises should spend the winter in a cool, well-lighted place where the temperature stays above freezing. Another reason to bring in the pines is so their containers don't crack in severe cold. The koi should also spend the winter indoors.

A simple teak bench, weathered gray, would be the best furniture for this garden of quiet pleasure, this haven of tranquil thought.

A Bonsai Garden

Because they are themselves so small, bonsai are ideal for little balconies or small terraces. A serenely Zen balcony might have three bonsai displayed on eye-level black plinths. Include a cascading pine so you'll have green the year around, a crabapple to bloom in spring, and a Japanese maple for autumn color and winter silhouette—each one is an evocation of the seasons.

The essence of bonsai is to capture the majesty of landscape, the power of nature, and a sense of great age in a tiny space. A bonsai suggests mountains, trees, the elements of nature, and the passing of time—just as William Blake's grain of sand represented a universe.

Bonsai are planted in specially made pots of several types. These include shallow trays; tiny teacuplike pots called *mame;* or deeper, often octagonal, pots. Some are glazed in cobalt blue, some in celadon green. Some are dark-brown unglazed clay. All are classically simple in design and unobtrusive in color. The plant should be selected first, then the pot chosen to complement the specimen. The pot is to the bonsai as a frame is to a picture: It should enhance, not distract.

Bonsai trees should look mature from the onset, so a comparatively thick trunk on a small tree is an asset. The five traditional styles of bonsai are determined by the shape or the angle of the trunk: formal upright, informal upright, slanting, semicascading, and cascading.

Left: Japanese maple (Acer palmatum) *is a favorite in Japanese-style gardens and adapts well to containers.*
Right: Apricot, cherry, and plum trees—all Prunus *species—are highly prized as flowering bonsai.*

Commonly used trees are Japanese trident maple (*Acer buergeranum*), Japanese beech (*Fagus japonica*), Japanese black pine (*Pinus thunbergiana*), and Japanese white pine (*Pinus parviflora*).

Bonsai subjects are divided into thirds: The bottom third displays the open trunk and partially exposed roots; the middle third emphasizes branch structure and the partially exposed trunk; and the top third, the division of main branches into branchlets and branchlets into tiny twigs. Branches are also arranged in groups of three. Of the three lowest branches, one is trained to the left, one to the right, and one to the back. One branch should be slightly higher than the other to achieve asymmetry. The branch at the back should fall between the other two. Branches should have space between them to give the effect of layers and to expose the shape of the trunk. A bonsai tree is usually densely branched and leaved at the top, to balance the pot visually.

The most treasured Japanese bonsai are naturally stunted trees found in the wild that show the effects of struggling against the elements. Thick, twisted trunks, windswept branches, and gnarled roots exposed over rough rocks are all highly valued. Young nursery-grown plants are trained with wire to achieve the effects that nature achieves with time, weather, and exposure. There are many books on the art of creating and growing bonsai. If you are a beginning bonsai gardener, sign up for a class at a community college or bonsai club. If you want to try on your own, watch a professional work at a bonsai nursery to get a

sense of the technique. Many nurseries mark down damaged, dwarfed, or irregularly branched trees that might serve well as bonsai subjects. Ask specifically to see discards when you are shopping.

Other plants besides trees can make very handsome bonsai specimens. Small-leaved kurume azaleas (*Rhododendron obtusum*) have the added bonus of providing flowers in the spring; cotoneaster (*Cotoneaster horizontalis* or *C. apiculatus*) has red berries through the winter; dwarf pomegranate (*Punica granatum* 'Nana') bears small, red fruits. A grove of bonsai trees always contains an uneven number— three, five, or seven. Japanese maples (*Acer palmatum* or *A. dissectum*), birch (*Betula* spp.), ginkgo (*Ginkgo biloba*), trident maple (*Acer buergeranum*), oak (*Quercus* spp.), zelkova, and Chinese elm all make fine bonsai forests.

Some bonsai are grown largely for their effect when in bloom. For this purpose, choices include apricot, azalea, camellia (*C. sasanqua*), carissa (*Carissa macrocarpa* 'Minima' or *C. grandiflora* 'Nana compacta'), cherry, crabapple, crape myrtle (*Lagerstroemia indica*), forsythia (*Forsythia viridissima* 'Bronxensis'), gardenia, jasmine, magnolia, osmanthus, peach, plum, quince, rhododendron, silk tree (*Grevillea robusta*), tea (*Camellia sinensis*), wintersweet (*Chimonanthus praecox*), and wisteria. For a succession of bloom in an outdoor room, these plants will bloom in approximately this order: apricot, forsythia, azalea, rhododendron, wisteria, crape myrtle, camellia, and gardenia.

Bonsai material that fruits includes cotoneaster, hawthorn, holly, and crabapple. Bonsai apple, pomegranate, and citrus trees all produce standard-sized fruit, though their trunk and leaf size are much smaller than normal.

Other bonsai are grown primarily for their fall foliage color and winter silhouette. Trees and shrubs native to North America are especially dramatic in full autumn foliage. For brilliant autumn leaves, look for barberry, beech, birch, Chinese elm, euonymus, ginkgo, hornbeam, Japanese maple, trident maple, oak, and zelkova.

For an evergreen winter display, choose cryptomeria (*Crytomeria japonica* 'Nana'), juniper (*Juniperus procumbens*), and a wide variety of pines—mugo pine (*Pinus mugo* var. *pumilo*), Japanese black pine (*P. thunbergi*), Japanese white pine (*P. pentaphylla*), or five-needled pine (*P. parviflora*).

For summer display, try dwarf fernleaf bamboo (*Arundinaria disticha*); golden willow; heavenly bamboo; tamarix; and even dwarf ornamental grasses, such as gold rattlesnake grass (*Briza minima*). Displayed near a pool or small waterfall, these look refreshingly cool on a hot summer's day.

Bonsai do best grown outdoors, but tender plants can easily be brought indoors for the winter in harsh-winter climates, so long as they are kept in a cool room. Even in the winter, bonsai must not be allowed to dry out completely. Flowering bonsai can be brought indoors briefly for display when they are in bloom, but the flowers will last longer if the pots go back outside at night. Blooming bonsai make a stunning centerpiece for a formal dinner or a striking accent in an entryway.

Sometimes a very small accent plant is grown in a separate bonsai pot as a companion piece to a larger bonsai. Plants that are naturally tiny, such as small ferns and alpines, work best for this. Some possible candidates as bonsai accent plants are alpine azalea (*Rhododendron lapponicum*), alpine buttercup (*Ranunculus eschscholtzii*), columbine (*Aquilegia canadensis*), bird's-foot violet (*Viola pedata*), blue-eyed-grass (*Sisyrinichium mucronatum*), blue violet (*Viola papilionacea*), bunchberry (*Cornus canadensis*), gold stargrass (*Hypoxis hirsuta*), horsetail (*Equisetum* spp.), mountain cranberry (*Vaccinium vitis-idaea* var. *minus*), pasture rose (*Rosa carolina*), par-

tridgeberry (*Mitchella repens*), shrubby cinquefoil (*Potentilla fruticosa*), trailing arbutus (*Epigaea repens*), saxifrage (*Saxifraga virginiensis*), wintergreen (*Gaultheria procumbens*), yellow violet (*Viola rotundifolia*), and small woodland ferns. Nurseries that specialize in native plants or alpines are likely places to find these species.

You may stumble across a plant that has never appeared on any list of potential bonsai materials but that is clearly destined for a bonsai pot in your outdoor room. Bougainvillea can make a stunning bonsai; so can a geranium or jade tree. When these unexpected felicities happen, adopt them gratefully and start looking for the perfect pot.

There's a world of ways to organize a collection of bonsai. You might collect only evergreens or only flowering bonsai. You might want to build or purchase special benches, one for each season. The bench on display could hold the most effective bonsai in turn. In winter, for example, the display bench could contain evergreen conifers, such as pine; berried plants, such as cotoneaster or holly; and paperbark maple, for its interesting bark texture and winter silhouette. The spring bench might burst into bloom all at once with bonsai azaleas or bonsai fruit trees. Or, the bench might feature a succession of bloom by presenting forsythia, rhododendron, wisteria, crape myrtle, and carissa. The summer bench could feature a simple round Japanese pot with a single waterlily and two brilliantly colored koi, set off by a golden willow bonsai and perhaps a companion piece of tall green equisetum. The autumn bench would have a group of bonsai—ginkgo, birch, and beech—as well as individual maple. The Japanese maple 'Sangu-Kaku' has bright red twigs that show beautifully after the autumn leaves have fallen. The autumn bench would present at least one chrysanthemum pruned and trained into a breathtaking cascade.

Furnish this outdoor room with a wooden bench or a few ceramic oriental garden seats. A small red lacquer table could hold a black iron Japanese teapot and a pair of delicately hand-painted Japanese teacups without handles. If the outdoor room is visible from the house and there is snow in winter, light a candle and place it in a stone snow lantern. End the day by watching the snow fall gently on the aged pines.

Left: Cactuses need a certain amount of space; they are easily damaged once their spiny protection has been breached.
Right: Prickly pear cactuses need exactly the right conditions to bloom.

SOUTHWEST STYLE

Drought-resistant, undemanding, with shapes and sizes of infinite variety, cactuses and succulents may be the most maintenance-free of all plants. To set a Southwestern mood, plant succulents in folk-art pots shaped like iguanas, tortoises, or coyotes. Rough-textured hand-thrown Mexican-style pots help carry out the theme, especially on a deck or terrace tiled with octagonal Mexican pavers.

Since sand is endemic to beaches as well as deserts, succulents in sand dunes can be the last word in low-maintenance gardening for a beach house. Where winters are warm, plant directly in the sand. Where they are cold, plant succulents in pots and, at summer's end, move them to a greenhouse, atrium, or house.

In a true desert climate, cactuses and succulents can be the most dramatic as well as the easiest way to landscape a deck or patio. Desert dwellers can grow the large sculptural cactuses such as prickly pear (*Opuntia*), escobaria, century plant (*Agave americana*) and *Agave attenuata*, giant club (*Cereus peruvianus* 'Monstrosus'), and elephant's-foot tree (*Beaucarnea recurvata*).

A Desert in the Air

Cactuses and succulents can be a godsend to the hurried, harried apartment dweller who wants an attractively landscaped balcony and can't imagine where to find the time to take care of it. This garden is about as no-fuss as a collection of living things can be. At one end of a sunny balcony, place a tall Mexican urn and plant it with queen's-wreath (*rosa de montana*, coral-vine, or *Antigonon leptopus*). Twine it over the railing and lace it in and out of the posts. It grows fast, covering the rail in dark-green heart-shaped leaves and sprays of rose-pink flowers, and is evergreen in warm climates. (Mulch the roots heavily in cold climates.) It's the only thing on this balcony that loves water, but a tall clay urn should keep the watering chores down to once a week, even in the summer. If the queen's-wreath outgrows the railing, train it on green string up the walls and along the edge of the ceiling to give the view a leafy frame—the plant can grow to 40 feet.

At the base of the railing, put a shallow planter (12 inches wide by 6 inches deep) the length of the balcony and fill it with a fast-draining planter mix. In it grow a collection of rosette-shaped succulents: pale green *Aeonium* 'Pseudotabulaeforme'; light green *A. urbicum;* blue-green red-edged *A. haworthii;* blue-green purple-edged hen-and-chickens (*Echeveria secunda* var. *glauca*); pale gray-green Mexican gem (*E. elegans*); ghostly white mother-of-pearl (*Graptopetalum paraguayense*); and, of *E. agavoides*, red-tinged green

molded-wax, pearly lavender-blue 'Perle von Nurnburg', luminous pink 'Morning Light', and deep maroon 'Black Prince'. Water them only when the soil is completely dry.

On the walls hang pots of white orchid cactus (*Epiphyllum*); fragrant white night-blooming cereus (*Hylocereus*); and, where there's plenty of room (or in a hanging basket), white queen-of-the-night (*Selenicereus grandiflorus*). Plant in a fast-draining soil and water only when completely dry.

In a hanging pot, grow wax-flower (*Hoya carnosa*). The summer flowers are fragrant round clusters of star-shaped pink and white flowers. The new leaves are red, though they eventually turn waxy green. Water wax-flower well in summer, then let the soil become mostly dry before watering again. Where temperatures drop below freezing, bring the plant indoors, where it makes a spectacular houseplant—just go easy on the water in winter, so the plant can go into dormancy. Don't prune wax-flower or cut the flowers: Next year's flowers bloom on the same ridged flower stubs.

Except for the queen's-wreath, this desertscape needs no pruning and minimal watering. Add a small, primitive Southwestern table and chairs, some brightly painted folk-art animals—a roadrunner, for example—and a geometrically patterned Navaho rug. Find a perforated tin lantern to add candlelight to the table. Now sit down. Kick off your shoes. Light the candle. Take a deep breath. Relax. Isn't it nice to be home?

The Succulent-Filled Terrace

A terrace or patio offers the option of using some of the big, bold, even grotesque cactuses and succulents to tremendous effect. Just don't use too many, or the effect is that of a horticultural freak show.

Remove the pavers in the center of a square patio and build a circular raised-bed planter that is 2 feet deep. Fill the planter with compost mixed liberally with gravelly sand. In the middle, plant a fairly large elephant's-foot tree (*Beaucarnea recurvata*). It has a weirdly swollen trunk base topped with long, thin curving leaves that look, depending on the observer, like either a cascading green fountain or an unruly ponytail. To one side, put in a desert-rose (*Adenium obesum*), which has a base, or caudex, almost as strange as the elephant's-foot tree. The desert-rose has long, shiny green leaves and clusters of brilliant red to pink flow-

Left: Where there is room for only one pot, a branching or columnar cactus can create the illusion of several plants.
Right: Epiphyllum are cactuses that have adapted to the forest. When in bloom, they are among the most spectacular of hanging plants.

Top: If you have a passion for succulents but your garden is small, consider displaying succulents on shelves designed for bonsai.
Center: Medusa's-head (Euphorbia caput-medusae) makes an appropriate planting in this container.
Bottom: The desert rose (Adenium obesum), which forms its own sculptural design as it grows, can be displayed as a bonsai.

ers in summer. The elephant's-foot tree is 20 feet tall at maturity; the desert-rose grows to 15 feet. To the other side, plant a group of three *Agave attenuata*. This agave is spineless and has soft translucent green leaves that will eventually spread to form a clump about 5 feet across. *A. attenuata* produces magnificently arching chartreuse flower spikes 12 to 14 feet long. In front of the clump, put in several *Dudleya brittoni*. This rosette-shaped succulent has luminous powdery-white leaves and grows to 18 inches across. In front of the desert-rose, plant *Agave victoriae-reginae,* which has beautifully patterned dark green leaves with bold white lines that emphasize its rosette shape. Fill in around these plantings with flat-growing *Aeonium tabuliforme,* a pale green rosette that is 12 inches in diameter at maturity.

To one side, behind the elephant's-foot tree, plant a crown of thorns (*Euphorbia milii*), which bears clusters of bright red bracts almost the year around. To the opposite side, plant a group of small sago palms (*Cycas revoluta*). When young, sago palms look like ferns; when mature, they look more like palms but they take many years to reach their mature height of 10 feet. In front of the sago palms, plant a *Dioscorea elephantipes,* which looks like a desert tortoise with a long, thin vine growing out of it. The vine has heart-shaped leaves and can grow as long as 30 feet. The tuber rarely gets more than about 2 feet wide. During its three- to four-month dormancy, its similarity to a hibernating tortoise is striking.

Fill in around these plants with cobweb houseleek and common houseleek (*Sempervivum arachnoideum, S. arachnoideum* 'Clara Noyes', and *S. tectorum*). Cobweb houseleek is a small, dense green rosette that appears to have a shining white cobweb woven over the top. 'Clara Noyes' is a deep-red variety. Common houseleek, also called hen-and-chickens, is a wide green rosette, often edged or tipped with purple. Where the ground-cover succulents—the sempervivums and the *Aeonium tabuliforme*—meet at either side, distribute them so there is no clear dividing line. They should seem to flow naturally, one into the other.

Obviously, this raised-bed planting is only for frost-free climates. It displays a variety of succulents worthy of the collector, yet all are reasonably easy to grow and reasonably easy to

acquire. It features trees, shrubs, and ground covers, as well as several plants with highly unusual and intriguing flowers. None of them has spines, except the crown-of-thorns. There is a great variety of foliage color, from dark green to pale green, from powdery white to red. There is structural interest in the caudexes of the elephant's-foot tree, desert-rose, and *Dioscorea elephantipes*. The repeated rosette motif gives the whole garden a sense of unity.

This garden does best when watered well and then allowed to dry out. Avoid watering plants much while they are dormant, usually in the winter. Succulents need water when leaf surfaces begin to shrivel slightly. Most succulents are remarkably pest-free, generally require little fertilizer, and rarely contract diseases unless they are overwatered. Dead or yellowed leaves need to be removed to keep the garden looking neat and tidy, but that's about all there is to do. The one area in which cactuses and succulents are uniformly unforgiving is injury: A break or scratch may heal over, but the result is an ugly scar for the life of the leaf or the plant.

Furnish this sunny terrace with a wooden table and chairs complete with a big market umbrella for welcome shade. In the early morning, dewdrops glitter on the cobweb houseleek. In the slanting rays of the afternoon sun, the *Agave attenuata* radiates a cool green translucence. And in the moonlight, the *Dudleya brittonii* glows as though lit from within.

The Spanish Courtyard

The traditional Spanish courtyard is essentially a high-walled patio. The privacy it gives, especially in an urban or suburban setting, is particularly precious in a world that often feels pressing and overcrowded. The classic architectural elements are thick adobe walls ornamented with ceramic tiles, Mexican pavers, a cascading fountain, and a filigreed wrought-iron gate under a red-tiled arch. The classic horticultural accoutrements provide a Mediterranean feeling: olives, figs, grapes, citrus, flowering vines, and rough clay pots of bright flowers or cool, green foliage.

Some courtyards face directly onto the street. Others are enclosed by the house. Although a central courtyard means less quiet and privacy for that part of the house that borders the sidewalk, it means that almost every room in the house can look out onto or open onto a garden. Long, overhanging eaves may shadow a verandah or arcade between the house and the courtyard itself, providing a place to sit in the shade or a scenic route from room to room.

Left: Agave attenuata grows to be quite large. Other agave species are much smaller. Right: Wall tiles, arches, and ornate ironwork evoke the Alhambra of Spain.

The front courtyard Through the black, elaborately patterned wrought-iron gate, the visitor sees only the large, tiered fountain, its waters cascading in a curtain of silver into a blue-tiled fish pond. The circular wall of the fish pond is wide enough to sit on to watch the darting goldfish or to trail fingers in the cool water. A few small white hardy waterlilies, *Nymphaea* 'Hermine', bloom on the surface. On the south wall, a tree that produces edible figs, 'Brown Turkey' (also called 'San Piero' or 'Black Spanish'), is espaliered. The figs must be picked when they ripen so they don't fall on the patio. And in autumn, after the huge, bold leaves fall, they must be raked. These tasks notwithstanding, the tree is exceptionally handsome against the whitewashed wall.

When pink bougainvillea 'Texas Dawn' or 'Pink Tiara' is trained to grow along the tops of the walls, the sense of enclosure and privacy will increase. Plant it in planters built into the wall, and fill the planters with topsoil or planter mix. Wall-grown bougainvillea needs pruning while it's flowering, to encourage heavier bloom. Simply trim off long stems for dramatic indoor bouquets; the vine will produce new wood and more flowers. Be especially cautious when transplanting bougainvillea—the rootballs have an unpleasant tendency to disintegrate when the pot is removed, and the consequences can be fatal for the plant. To remove rootballs safely, slice the plastic pots with a razor knife; slide the plant, pot and all, into the planting hole; and gently wiggle the pot off the rootball.

For a genuinely authentic note, place a pair of matching tall clay urns next to the wrought-iron gate and plant in them the famous 'Rose of Castile' of the Spanish missions. This damask rose is also known as *Rosa damascena* 'Autumn Damask'. It flowers twice a year in loose, fragrant clusters, and its 6-foot canes can be trained over the gate. Place a matching pair of roses at the entry to the house.

At one corner, remove pavers to make room for an olive tree, *Olea europaea* 'Swan Hill'. 'Swan Hill' is reliably fruitless, which means there are no little, inedible black olives to stain the courtyard. Olive trees have silvery gray, willow-like leaves and picturesquely gnarled trunks. Unlike most trees, olives transplant well when mature: To get the sense of grace and graciousness that an aged olive con-

tributes to a garden, buy the biggest, oldest tree you can afford. Olives grow slowly, and planting a young one can mean never seeing the courtyard cooled by its leaves, though your grandchildren may one day sit under its shade.

In the planter beneath the wall opposite the espaliered fig, put in star-jasmine and train it up the wall. Pinch new shoots to control height, and direct the growth in the direction you want it to go. The small, fragrant white flowers will scent the summer air deliciously.

This is not a low-maintenance landscape. The roses, the fig, the star-jasmine, and the bougainvillea all need pinching or pruning once a year. They must also be tied and trained on the walls. The figs must be picked before they drop, and the fruit must be protected from the birds if family and friends are to have any. Fallen fig leaves must be raked in the fall. The roses may need spraying. The bougainvillea and waterlilies may need fertilizer. The fountain must be kept clear of algae, and fish need to be fed daily.

On the other hand, such a courtyard is a landscape for the ages. All these plants will live for many years, growing more beautiful each year. The garden offers flowers almost the year around and provides a flamboyant burst of bloom in early summer. The air is sweetly scented by the damask roses, the star-jasmine, and the waterlilies. This is a delightful place to sit under the olive tree on a summer afternoon—savoring the sweetness of the air, listening to the cascading water, and watching the ripples dance in the sunlight.

The interior courtyard Given a courtyard with a thick, whitewashed adobe wall on one side and the house forming the other three sides, plant a blue-flowered jacaranda (*Jacaranda mimosifolia*) in the center of the courtyard. Around it build a tile-and-adobe bench to sit on, leaving plenty of room for the trunk to grow thicker. Jacaranda has exquisite blue flowers in spring or summer and lacy, fernlike leaves through which the sun filters softly. On the tree the flowers are breathtaking; even after they have fallen, they look so lovely when scattered on the patio you may hate to sweep them up.

Creeping fig (*Ficus pumila*) can be planted to climb the wall. Delicate in appearance, yet sturdy, self-clinging, and evergreen, creeping

This mosaic tiling is spectacular and worth the effort of installation.

fig bears almost no resemblance to its better-known cousins, the trees. It will someday bear figs on mature growth, but the fruits are inedible and the mature growth much less appealing than the juvenile leaves, so trim out mature branches as they appear. (It usually takes years before any do.)

While the creeping fig is creeping its way up the wall, hang wrought-iron pot holders and fill them with pots of garden geraniums (*Pelargonium × hortorum*), regal geraniums (*P. × domesticum*), and ivy geranium (*P. peltatum*). The possible colors range from the classic crayon-red to pink, rose, red, violet, lavender, magenta, and white. They grow best with lots of sun (geraniums get leggy and tatty in the shade), rich fast-draining soil, regular pinching to make them dense and bushy, and deadheading to keep new flowers coming. They bloom

best when they are slightly pot bound, so check them frequently to make sure they're getting enough water, since there's not much extra soil to retain moisture. During the height of summer, they may need watering almost daily. Fancy-leaf or colored-leaf common geraniums have intricately patterned leaves almost as striking as their flowers. One or the other of these three species will be in bloom almost all year in mild-winter climates.

Look into the garden from the house and see a long wall of brightly blooming pots of geraniums softened by the tracery of the creeping fig; the delicate, fernlike leaves of the jacaranda; and the flamboyance of exquisite blue jacaranda flowers. A pair of wooden garden benches, one at either end, would make it easy to enjoy the sunshine and the shade in this pleasant and private interior courtyard.

TROPICAL SPACES

In southern Florida, along the Gulf Coast, and in Hawaii, Puerto Rico, the U.S. Virgin Islands, and southern California, decks and patios are likely to be replaced by a covered lanai. The covering protects those beneath it from intense sun and torrential rains, and the space is often screened to protect its inhabitants from no-see-ums. Lanais call for a style of landscaping that is completely different from that of garden or balcony. In a lanai, temperate-zone annuals would bloom themselves out and die of exhaustion in a few weeks. The lack of significant temperature variation means that classic favorites such as roses, peonies, and apple trees won't thrive. The existence of an arbor or roof limits the use of trees.

Tropical plants are famous for their voracious growth: 6 inches high the day they're planted, 6 feet high in what seems like no time at all. Lanais need to be planted with subtropical and tropical species that won't take over between noon and suppertime.

A staghorn fern and donkey's-tail, a succulent, add a wild and exotic note.

Because the weather is so often balmy, the lanai can be used as an outdoor room almost every day of the year, and it is likely to be furnished more like an interior room than most decks and patios. This is where bamboo or rattan furniture really comes into its own, where the cushion fabrics are more likely to feature hibiscus and parrots than chintz peonies or paisley prints.

An Arbor-Covered Lanai

Over the arbor grow wonga-wonga vine (*Pandorea pandorana*), Madagascar jasmine (*Stephanotis floribunda*), and orchid-vine (*Stigmaphyllon ciliatum*). The wonga-wonga vine is a handsome, glossy vine with pale pink trumpet-shaped flowers. It grows in either sun or shade and with a minimum of water once it's established. White-flowered Madagascar jasmine is the richly fragrant stephanotis of bridal bouquets. Orchid-vine has clusters of flowers that closely resemble oncidium orchids (although they are not at all related), and it features delicate, heart-shaped foliage. All three vines are evergreen in mild climates and bloom from summer into fall.

Along the sides of the lanai, put in a hibiscus hedge of soft pink 'Amour' and white 'Bridal Veil' hibiscus (*Hibiscus rosa-sinensis*). Both grow to 10 feet in height but can be kept lower with pruning. Prune height by about one-third in early spring, and pinch out tips of stems spring through summer to get more flowers.

At the outer corners of the arbor, plant or pot a matched pair of Australian tree ferns (*Cyathea cooperi*). In the dappled shade of the arbor, put pots of sago palm (*Cycas*), white lily-flowered *Spathiphyllum* 'Mauna Loa', and one large pot planted with Abyssinian banana (*Ensete ventricosum* 'Maurelii'). Abyssinian banana has huge, dramatic, banana-tree leaves and dark red stalks. On the walls of the arbor, hang big staghorn ferns (*Platycerium bifurcatum*) and small bromeliads. The collector or serious gardener may want to add epiphytic jungle orchids grown on bark. A local orchid society can put you in touch with knowledgeable orchid growers and sources. From the top of the arbor, hang baskets of white-striped spider plant (*Chlorophytum comosum* var. *vittatum*).

Furnished with airy rattan tables and chairs, this lanai would be a lovely place to enjoy the cool breezes and dappled sunlight of the arbor.

Left: Banana tree
Right: Spathiphyllum
with its floral spike
visible

The hibiscus hedges make the space seem very private, the vines shade the arbor, the spathiphyllum bloom, and the Australian tree ferns add a tropical grace to the whole lanai.

A Tropical Fragrance Garden

Next to a sunny lanai, plant an ylang-ylang (*Cananga odorata*) tree. Its sweetly fragrant, showy yellow flowers bloom the year around and are the source of one of the essential essences in making perfumes. It grows slowly, to 40 feet in full sun, and prefers to be kept moist at the roots. One tree will perfume an entire garden.

Edge the lanai with a low hedge of natal plum (*Carissa grandiflora* 'Boxwood Beauty') 2 feet high and 2 feet wide. Carissa has white star-shaped flowers very like star-jasmine, with a surprisingly similar fragrance the year around.

Trellised up one side of the lanai, plant Chilean jasmine (*Mandevilla laxa*), a deciduous vine that twines to 15 feet and higher. It has clusters of white trumpet-shaped flowers that smell like gardenias all summer long.

In a large tub or pot, plant harlequin glorybower (*Clerodendrum trichotomum*). A deciduous shrub or small tree that can eventually grow to 15 feet, it has soft, furry dark-green leaves and fragrant clusters of red and white tubular flowers. The scarlet calyxes hang on after the petals have dropped and contrast beautifully with the shiny turquoise fruit.

In another large tub, plant orange jessamine (*Murraya paniculata*). It can be grown as a small, airy evergreen tree with gracefully draping branches; glossy, dark green leaves; and white bell-shaped flowers that smell like jasmine. It blooms from summer through fall

A bromeliad Neoregelia
carolinae

and sometimes in the springtime, too. Put it where it gets filtered shade or morning sun.

In a third pot, plant a gardenia (*Gardenia jasminoides* 'August Beauty'). Like the jasmine for which it is named, *G. jasminoides* is famous for its intensely fragrant white flowers. 'August Beauty' has glossy bright green leaves and large double flowers, and the plant blooms heavily from May to November.

This perfumed garden offers flowers and fragrance every month of the year. Unlike most tropical gardens, it has no flamboyant, neon-colored flowers, no rampant vines, no huge leaves, no sense of being overwhelmed by the jungle. It is orderly and restrained, a study in the simplicity of green and white, with flowers that sweeten the air with rich perfumes. If the healing claims of aromatherapy have any truth to them, all you have to do to achieve better health in this garden is to breathe.

Raised beds increase garden accessibility and allow sit-down gardening.

THE ACCESSIBLE GARDEN

There may come a time when your protesting back tells you that a day of gardening is no longer sufficient compensation for the aches and pains and stiffness. Growing older or losing mobility is not a reason to give up the joy of gardening, however. All it means is that you need to go about it a little differently.

A Design for Convenience

Raised planters that require no bending, squatting, or kneeling can make gardening a pure pleasure once again. Decks and patios are especially well suited to thoughtfully designed planters that enhance the deck or patio while providing plenty of planting space. Custom wooden planters can be built to a height appropriate for the gardener. They can be deep, solid planters filled with soil, or fairly wide beds with space underneath, or a series of tiered shelves for potted plants. Potting tables, too, can be made to the appropriate height as can storage for extra pots, soil amendments, plant ties, stakes, and similar essentials.

An arbor over the deck or patio allows sun and shade, accommodating a wide range of plants. The area under the arbor might be given over to ornamentals; the sunny spaces can be devoted to vegetables. A drip-trickle system can eliminate the need to lug around a heavy watering can. A wheeled cart can make it easy to move bags of potting soil without heavy lifting. Vines—such as scarlet runner bean, tomato, or passionflower—grown up posts from raised beds can produce flowers and fruit at eye level instead of 2 feet off the ground.

A patio can have waist-high raised beds as easily as a deck. Build redwood boxes 18 inches deep and an arm's length wide (no more than 3 feet). Place the boxes on sturdy 2 by 4 frames of the same dimensions, line them with 6-mil plastic stapled inside, and fill the boxes with topsoil. This is easier said than done—it can take an experienced carpenter a weekend or two. If you are the gardener whose back is inclined to creak, hire a high school student or grandchild to help.

If the patio attaches to the house, have the planters built on the remaining three sides. Beneath the planters grow meadowsweet (*Astilbe*) and small woodland ferns, both of which thrive in moist shade. The low-growing ground covers baby's-tears (*Soleirolia soleirolii*) and Corsican mint (*Mentha requienii*) would also do well under the planters.

Almost anything that can grow in the garden can grow in planters this big, with the exception of full-sized trees and large shrubs. The gardener who enjoys constantly changing effects and showy displays might plant a different combination for each season, trying out new variations each year. The suburban farmer or serious cook might plant a salad garden on one side, an herb garden on another, and an orchard of genetic dwarf fruit trees on the third. The keen collector could fit in a substantial collection of plants with one planter each devoted to one or several species or genus.

Whatever the effect you choose—from the sweet "disorder" of a cottage garden to the neatly laid-out rows of the vegetable plot, from the collector's specialties to the miniature orchard—the critical point is that you can take pleasure in using these planters long after most garden maintenance has been turned over to the child next door or the weekly landscaping service.

WONDROUS WATER GARDENS

Wall fountains with recirculating pumps are available in stores that specialize in garden ornaments. Some garden centers also offer prefabricated kits for building redwood-sided pools with small fountain jets. Nurseries that specialize in water-garden plants typically offer pool kits, fountain heads, fountains, drains, filters, submersible pumps, underwater lights, water sealants, and other necessary supplies. For information and materials, write to Lilypons Water Gardens, 6800 Lilypons Road, Box 10, Buckeystown, MD 21717-0010 or Van Ness Water Gardens, 2460 North Euclid Avenue, Upland, CA 91786-1199.

For most gardeners, the building of a fountain, stream, or waterfall is best left to the expert, preferably a contractor with plenty of experience. Water can be difficult to manage; it is inclined to go its own way. When this waywardness exhibits itself in the form of a crack or a leak, it can be enormously frustrating to find and fix. However, once installed and working properly, few garden elements are as pleasurable and rewarding.

Though calling a professional is usually the best course when it comes to decorative elements that use running water, the construction of a garden pool in a container is something most people can do—provided they follow a few guidelines. If you are considering a garden pool, your first job is to find out if your balcony or deck can support the weight of a pond. Do this *before* investing in tubs, soil, sand, plants, and fish.

Figuring the weight of water in a container involves two steps: figuring the volume of the water—that is, the number of gallons—and then multiplying the number of gallons by the weight of water per gallon. The formula for figuring the number of gallons for a round tub is $3.14 \times (0.5 \text{ diameter} \times 0.5 \text{ diameter}) \times \text{depth}$. Make sure the measurements are in feet or fractions of a foot; this will give you the number of cubic foot. There are 7.5 gallons of water per cubic feet; therefore, multiply the number of cubic feet by 7.5 to get the number of gallons the circular container holds. For a rectangular tub, the formula is length × width × depth. Remember to measure in feet or fractions of a foot to get the number of cubic feet. Once again, multiply the number of cubic feet by 7.5

to determine the number of gallons of water. Water weighs 8 pounds per gallon. To find the weight of the water, multiply the number of gallons by 8.

If the container will be home to fish, your next job is to determine how many fish the water in the container can support. The traditional guideline allows 15 inches of fish per square yard of surface area. That means one 15-inch fish, two 7-inch fish, or five 3-inch fish per square yard.

The next task is to consider contaminants. If your container will be a half-barrel that once held wine, whiskey, or olives, take the precautions cited in the design called The Condominium Tub Garden. Precautions are also necessary in regard to the water-purification chemicals

High-gushing fountains need powerful pumps. The volume of water to be pumped, the distance the water must travel from the pump, and the height of the spray should determine pump capacity.

*Japanese koi bring
color and motion
to the garden.*

that local water districts add to water. These chemicals can kill fish. Find out from your water district what chemicals are used in your area. The steps you need to follow to prepare the water for fish are described in the next paragraph.

If the water in your area contains chlorine, fill the tub and let the water sit for a day or two before adding the fish. The chlorine will dissipate naturally. If the water in your area contains chloramine, a combination of chlorine and ammonia, you must treat the water with chemicals to make it safe for fish. Fish stores and water-garden suppliers sell the necessary chemicals. Treat the water between 8:00 and 10:00 in the morning, when the oxygen supply is at its peak. Once a tub is established, you may be able to add small amounts of untreated water (a maximum of 5 percent of the volume of the tub) without causing harm, but consult with a local fish supplier before trying it.

Even when swimming in decontaminated water, your fish won't be safe unless you have provided them with protection from predators. The predator list provided by Lilypons Water Gardens includes raccoons, fish-eating birds

(herons, egrets, kingfishers, and the like), cats, turtles, water snakes, and frogs. Cats and raccoons are the most likely predators in urban and suburban situations. You can thwart them by securing hardware cloth an inch below the surface of the water. Cut the hardware cloth to size with wire cutters, or have the staff at the hardware store where you buy the cloth do it for you. If your tub is made of wood, bend the cloth and staple it into place. If the container is ceramic or metal, bend the wire over the edge to hold the screen firmly in position. Under the surface of water, wire barely shows at all. Plants can grow through the spaces, and predators won't be able to get to the flora or the fauna.

When you buy fish, find out whether the species you have chosen is likely to nibble at the plants in the pond. If so, you may have to provide wire plant protectors. You can buy these or make your own by bending a piece of chicken wire to form a cage over each plant. In time, the plant will grow right through it.

Constructing a water garden does take planning. Consider this compensation, however: The well-planned pond is practically main-

tenance-free. Water snails are the gardeners in the tub garden; they eat the algae. Aquatic snails include ramshorn, papershell, cornucopia, Columbia, African ear horn, and black Japanese species. The fish help police the habitat: They eat algae and pests (mosquito larvae, aphids, flies, and other undesirables). Some species eat excess plant material. In the well-planned pond, the fish won't even need to be fed.

The Condominium Tub Garden

Few condominiums offer their residents much more gardening space than a concrete patio or a balcony. A half-barrel, an oriental ceramic planter, a large stone crock, or even an old clawfoot tub can make a fine water garden for a confined space.

Old barrels often contain bacteria that can harm plants or fish, even after they've been charred, and redwood containers can discolor water. If you're using a half-barrel that once held wine, whiskey, or olives, staple a 4- by 5-foot PVC lining to the wood. The PVC lining will prevent problems. If you're using a clawfoot tub, haul it to a sunny place where you can leave it permanently. (For this tub garden, five to six hours of sun per day is ideal.) Once the tub is filled with sand and water, it will be much too heavy to even consider moving.

Fill the container halfway with topsoil or sandy loam. Do not use potting mix, compost, peat, or steer manure. Plant one hardy waterlily. Choice selections are white 'Hermine'; pale pink 'Fabiola'; yellow 'Marliacea Chromatella'; and the 'Paul Hariot', which changes colors from canary yellow to pink to scarlet as it matures. These do well in tubs, bloom profusely, and are extremely hardy in zones 3 through 10.

Place the lily tuber at a 45-degree angle in the center of the tub. Add two to four bunches of oxygenating plants to help maintain a healthy oxygen balance. Effective oxygenating plants are *Cabomba, Myriophyllum,* and *Sagittaria sinensis.* Off to the side, plant the white iris 'Her Highness' and the lavender and white iris 'Bryce Leigh'. 'Her Highness' blooms through the spring; the 'Bryce Leigh', in the early summer.

Once the plants are firm in the soil, add ½ inch of sand. Pull an old sock over the end of the hose, to prevent soil and water from splash-

ing out of the tub, and slowly add water to within 2 inches of the top. When you purchase your plants, purchase aquatic plant fertilizer tablets as well; the nursery staff will be able to tell you exactly how much to add and how frequently, based on the size of the tub.

Because water temperatures are more variable in a small tub than in a large pond or in-ground water container, goldfish and koi (*Cyprinus carpio*) may not do well in the tub described in this design. Better choices might be mosquito fish (*Gambusia*) or guppies. Consult the staff at the place you buy the fish. Ask about water volume, water temperature, hours of sunlight, and water plants.

Goldfish (*Carassius auratus*) and koi may nibble on the submerged plants as well as on the algae, to the serious detriment of the plants. If necessary, provide wire plant protectors so the submerged plants can survive the attentions of the fish. Or, put in golden orfe, fish that, like trout, feed on insects at the surface and leave plants alone. Remember to add water snails to minimize maintenance. For a half-barrel, you'll need six snails.

To complete the landscaping of the condominium patio, plant the walls with self-clinging vines to create a place of green leafiness. Add a cast-aluminum reproduction of a cast-iron Victorian garden bench and surround it with fern fronds, grapevines, and morning glories. Cover it with plump, flowered cushions on which you can sit in the early morning and contemplate the perfection of the waterlily; the elegance of the iris; and the shining, sinuous fish.

Chinese water chestnut, lotus, and watercress make an edible tub garden.

The Patio Pool

A more spacious patio can accommodate a more spacious water garden. In England, old stone horse troughs are much sought after for water gardens. In the United States, an inexpensive but substantial container is a galvanized stock tank of the sort used for watering horses or cattle. Use an oval stock tank 4 feet long, 2 feet wide (30 inches wide in the center), and 12 inches deep or a circular tank 4 feet in diameter. The tank can be set directly on the patio or, if that would take up too much room, sunk in the soil adjacent to the patio.

If the tank is set on the patio, mask the tank by banking it on all sides with terra-cotta pots of calla lilies, large ferns, and irises. To bury the tank, leave a margin of 2 feet from the patio and dig a hole in which to sink the tank to within 1 inch of the surface of the soil. Hide the edges by planting low-growing ground covers such as Irish moss, Kenilworth ivy, or creeping blue-star (*Isotoma*). The dilemma is this: Water gardens need five to six hours of sun for the waterlilies to bloom; most of the plants

This arrangement of rocks brings nature right to the edge of the pool. The patio provides access and space to study the reflections.

that thrive near water prefer filtered shade. If the tank does not receive direct midday sun, plant the edges with hostas, sweet violets, and low-growing ferns. If the tank does get full sun, plant variegated sweetflag (*Acorus calamus* var. *variegata*), sweetflag (*A. calamus*), yellow water iris (*Iris pseudacorus*), and double yellow water iris (*Iris pseudoacorus* 'Flora Plena'). Plant *Mentha* species, or mint species, as ground covers, and keep the surrounding soil moist. Because mint is inclined to spread enthusiastically by underground runners, it's wise to sink it in pots to keep the roots confined. When mint gets tatty, shear it, and let it come back with fresh, new growth.

Once the tank is sunk and a plan devised for planting the margins, fill the tank half full with topsoil. Use plastic or pulp pans to plant the water plants. Once planted, add a ½-inch layer of sand or pea gravel at the top to keep the soil from muddying the water. In a 16-inch dark plastic tub, plant one lotus. Lotus tubers come sprouted, looking rather like bananas laid end to end, and they are very brittle—handle them

gently. The thickest part of the tuber should be covered with 2 inches of soil, with its growing tip ½ inch above the soil. Best choices for tank gardens are yellow tulip lotus (*Nelumbo nucifera* 'Shirokunihi'), deep rose 'Momo Botan', and pink and cream 'Chawan Basu'.

Lotuses take a year to get established; they bloom the second year. The blossoms open in the morning and close in the afternoon and bloom for six to eight weeks starting in June or July. The petals fall open the third day, revealing the intriguingly shaped seedpod. The fragrance is legendary, as you will remember if you reread Homer's *Odyssey.*

In a 13-inch pan, plant a tropical waterlily. Tropical waterlilies come in spectacular blues in addition to the whites, pinks, and reds of hardy waterlilies. *Nymphaea* 'Colorata' is a small day-blooming tropical lily that blooms profusely in wisteria blue. The rich deep-blue 'Mrs. Martin E. Randig' is another fine choice. Both of these are extremely fragrant. They will survive the winter outdoors in zone 10 but must be brought indoors for the winter elsewhere.

Plant another 13-inch tub with one hardy waterlily: white 'Hermine'; pale pink 'Fabiola'; yellow 'Marliacea Chromatella'; or 'Paul Hariot', with its day-to-day shifts from canary yellow to pink and from yellow to scarlet as it matures. To complete the tub, place pots of white bog lily (*Crinum americanum*) and Egyptian papyrus (*Cyperus papyrus*) at the back of the tank as a background for the waterlilies. Remember to figure out the number of scavenger snails and submerged oxygenating plants you need—you can consult with the water-plant nursery staff.

Obviously, in a larger tank you can have larger fish. Practice first with inexpensive goldfish (*Carassius auratus*), which are fascinating in themselves: These include the comets, shubunkins, Japanese fantails, calicoes, and orandas. If these prove satisfactory and satisfying, consider adding some Japanese koi—the name means brocaded carp. The colors of koi (*Cyprinus carpio*) are extraordinary: metallic gold, silver, and copper; blue, red, yellow, orange, and platinum; many koi have two or three colors. These fish are extremely hardy; surprisingly easy to keep once the tank is clear and ecologically balanced; and can be trained, as they have been at the Allerton Gardens in Kauai and at the Imperial Palace in Kyoto, to

A night-blooming waterlily, Nymphaea *'Hylocereus'*

come at a handclap. They don't need to be fed every day, they're quiet, they never need to be walked, and they live for many years.

This tank, whether the 4-foot oval or the 4-foot circle, is a relatively easy, comparatively inexpensive way to have the joys of water in an outdoor room. The tropical waterlilies and lotus are richly fragrant and wonderfully different from other garden flowers. The irises and bog lilies have their own exquisite flowers. The papyrus plants add yet another graceful note of the exotic. The snails and the fish should do most of the garden work, although you will need to bring the tender plants indoors before the first frost. The movement and brilliant colors of the fish are a constant delight.

Furnish this patio with bent-willow tables and big chairs—the tables at which to eat, the chairs from which to survey the garden. Take pleasure in the heady fragrance of the waterlilies; the perfect form of the lotus, both flower and pod; and the ripples of water that betray the swirl of the imperial koi. Water is inherently soothing; it eases the heart, and brings tranquility to the mind. And, is that not, after all, the purpose of a garden?

U.S. Measure and Metric Measure Conversion Chart

	Symbol	When you know:	Multiply by:	To find:	Rounded Measures for Quick Reference		
Mass (weight)	oz	ounces	28.35	grams	1 oz		= 30 g
	lb	pounds	0.45	kilograms	4 oz		= 115 g
	g	grams	0.035	ounces	8 oz		= 225 g
	kg	kilograms	2.2	pounds	16 oz	= 1 lb	= 450 g
					32 oz	= 2 lb	= 900 g
					36 oz	= 2¼ lb	= 1000 g (1 kg)
Volume	pt	pints	0.47	liters	1 c	= 8 oz	= 250 ml
	qt	quarts	0.95	liters	2 c (1 pt)	= 16 oz	= 500 ml
	gal	gallons	3.785	liters	4 c (1 qt)	= 32 oz	= 1 liter
	ml	milliliters	0.034	fluid ounces	4 qt (1 gal)	= 128 oz	= 3¾ liter
Length	in.	inches	2.54	centimeters	⅜ in.		= 1 cm
	ft	feet	30.48	centimeters	1 in.		= 2.5 cm
	yd	yards	0.9144	meters	2 in.		= 5 cm
	mi	miles	1.609	kilometers	2½ in.		= 6.5 cm
	km	kilometers	0.621	miles	12 in. (1 ft)		= 30 cm
	m	meters	1.094	yards	1 yd		= 90 cm
	cm	centimeters	0.39	inches	100 ft		= 30 m
					1 mi		= 1.6 km
Temperature	° F	Fahrenheit	$\frac{5}{9}$ (after subtracting 32)	Celsius	32° F		= 0° C
	° C	Celsius	$\frac{9}{5}$ (then add 32)	Fahrenheit	212° F		= 100° C
Area	in.²	square inches	6.452	square centimeters	1 in.²		= 6.5 cm²
	ft²	square feet	929.0	square centimeters	1 ft²		= 930 cm²
	yd²	square yards	8361.0	square centimeters	1 yd²		= 8360 cm²
	a.	acres	0.4047	hectares	1 a.		= 4050 m²

Formulas for Exact Measures   Rounded Measures for Quick Reference